Thine Adversaries Roar ...

IN MEMORIAM

The Very Reverend C. Patrick Hankey
Dean of Ely
1950–1970

Thine Adversaries Roar . . .

Autobiographical observations
1922–1999

Michael Howard
formerly Organist, Ely Cathedral

First published in 2001

Gracewing
2 Southern Avenue
Leominster
Herefordshire HR6 0QF

© Michael Howard 2001

ISBN 0 85244 530 X

Typesetting by
Action Publishing Technology Ltd, Gloucester, GL1 1SP

Printed in England by MPG Books Ltd.,
Bodmin PL31 1EG

Contents

'Were such things here, as we doe speake about?
Or have we eaten on the insane Root,
That takes the Reason Prisoner?'
(Macbeth)

Foreword

by Peter Giles

Ely was a vibrant place during the 1950s. This was due in no small measure to the inspiration of the priestly Dean Patrick Hankey, and the dynamism of Michael Howard's choir. Ely Cathedral is huge, two-towered, stunning, and possesses a superb acoustic. When I was there it had a feeling of satisfying musical and liturgical correctness and a clear Anglo-Catholic bias.

The repertoire was almost totally English: virtually nothing was sung from outside English cathedral/Chapel Royal tradition, 12th century onwards. There was therefore nothing from oratorios or anything written for a mixed-voice choir, and there were no 'arrangements'. The repertoire was restricted to absolute quality (which resulted in a rather limited Victorian/Edwardian presence), and it was also modest-sized to allow for thorough preparation and, therefore, a worthy performance-offering. Newer – that is, contemporary works – were carefully spaced because they are disproportionately time-consuming to prepare. The only daily hymn was the correct office-hymn, to plainsong. Latin motets were never performed in English. In Ely, of course, there was absolutely no question of using an English translation. In services which were accompanied, nothing was included which was originally written for strings or orchestra. The inevitable preclusion was Purcell's verse anthems with string band.

All this may sound negative, but don't be deceived: there was a fresh, *positive* feel in the fens! The choral sound from the sixteen choristers and eight lay clerks was electrifying. Diction was not merely considered important. Words were there to glory in. The boys' voices had a strong, exciting timbre. Ely produced James Bowman, Grayston Ives, and Nigel Perrin, to name but three notable ex-choristers.

Howard's 'Ely Sound' was famous for those days; much broadcast and recorded, it was to prove influential. Correct movement and manner were considered imperative to the aesthetic offering being made. No talking, loud or otherwise, was permitted in procession – even out of sight of the congregation – by canons, lay-clerks and choristers alike, before or after service until inside the sound-proof vestries. The Daily Office – the *Opus Dei* was sacrosanct. Never was the time of Evensong shifted to allow for, say, a concert rehearsal. Extra events were considered strictly extra.

Services at Ely felt monastic and esoteric. They were as far from populist as it is possible to imagine.

PETER GILES
Chairman, Campaign for the Defence
of the Traditional Cathedral Choir

Preface I

The Ely Sound

There will doubtless be those who in reading this book hope to find the 'magic formula', coupled with a step-by-step analysis, as to how the Ely sound of the Michael Howard era was created, with the laudable intention of emulating it. Those looking for a dispassionate system, clinically applied, will be disappointed, for they will find no set of rules and procedures which guarantees success. But the clues are there for those who seek. The key is the *Opus Dei* – the whole essence of worship 'for the greater glory of God'. There was a preciousness to every service as if it had never happened before and might never happen again.

Like all church music, the Ely Sound had its roots in the worship of God absolutely; the music was not just prepared and then presented to a high standard, rather it was, on each occasion, interpreted. As with the sermon on a well-known text, so it was that the music was re-interpreted for that unique occasion. It demanded a sensitivity not only to the place but also to the occasion and indeed to the choir itself. With the timelessness that was almost tangible, the links with the monastic past proved the Psalmist's point 'a thousand years in Thy sight are but as yesterday.'

Michael Howard writes of himself with, at times, a brutal honesty but with great humility: his is a pilgrimage with an underlying sense of God's calling. There are many of us who shared that part of the journey with him and will ever be grateful for his vision and certainty in the things that mattered most, as well as being inspired to put into practice what we had learned and absorbed. In the book he writes of his relationship with his choristers as *primus inter pares*. For us he was simply the leader of the pack, ever adventurous and exciting in his vision, never content with less than the best, yet capable of enabling us to achieve it. Without doubt he was demanding, but he was a leader rather than a driver. No mean singer himself, he would demonstrate and inspire. Always there was a sense of urgency not just because practice time was precious, but because the task was vital.

Those who aspire to anything like the Ely sound of Michael Howard's era will be those for whom worship is the most important calling. Those who do not share this or who do not reach for a vision of Heaven, cannot begin to achieve it. A cathedral choir is not just a group of highly-skilled performers, but a vital part of a community whose *raison d'etre* is the worship of Almighty God. 'It is the Spirit that giveth life.'

The Reverend Jonathan Boston
Litcham Rectory
Norfolk

Preface II

An Ely Chorister Remembers ...

When Michael was appointed Organist and Magister Choristarum at Ely I had been in the choir some three years and was Head Chorister. He was certainly different to his predecessors. He spent a lot of time on vocal exercises which at first we found less enjoyable than singing real music. However Michael made them fun and often brought his lovely Samoyed bitch Anna to practices. She was much loved by us boys who when at boarding school had no animals of our own. Anyone who cared for his dog as Michael did could not be bad!

At first it was not popular when Stanford and Parry were removed from the music lists, but it was clear that Michael knew what he was about and was determined to improve the choir. In due course we noticed that the strange exercises were projecting and focusing the sound we made and Michael revealed to us the depth of beauty in the Tudor composers with works like Byrd's *Ave verum* and an anonymous 'Rejoice in the Lord alway.' He took the greatest trouble to see that what we sang was 'of the best', and so we painstakingly and slowly learned the plainsong Office Hymns for the day. The sound of the boys singing alone in that wonderful building with pure and restrained organ accompaniment will always be with me. Also music by Cornysh, Taverner and others was introduced, all hand written on large manuscript paper. We were breaking new ground.

The experience of all this has been a life enduring joy, and when the time came that I could sing treble no longer, I went to Michael. He with typical kindness said 'I want you to help me in the organ loft' – and so I gained an insight into what one does to accompany a choir.

What we did not realise until later was that Michael was a leader as a cathedral organist, ahead of his time. He was one of the first to conduct his choir and to get his assistant to play – the result being much better co-ordination and control. Furthermore, his ability to train boys to sing with a bright, unique tone was only equalled by one or two of his contemporaries.

But it was in the area of authentic performance that Michael played such a vital part. Few people are aware that without his work with the Renaissance Singers we should not be where we are today. So we have a truly remarkable man. Who else would have resigned from Tewkesbury Abbey to go off and start a new choir in the middle of the war, in a London which was being bombed!

Howard Thomas
Organist, Wymondham Abbey
Norfolk

Introduction and Acknowledgements

The substance of all contained in this book has been fermenting and progressively developing in my mind in the course of the last forty years. What I might call a point of detonation was reached during 1998 by my reading of the Reverend Philip Barrett's *Barchester*, and also certain essays in the collection *Faking It*, assembled by Dr Digby Anderson and the Reverend Peter Mullen. The final point of explosion was brought about by the decimating programme gradually revealed by the present Government facing an Opposition party already divided against itself. Everything that I have been impelled to say stems not merely from observance, but from my direct experience as a professional musician.

The year 1999 saw the four hundred and fiftieth anniversary of the Book of Common Prayer, that masterpiece of incomparable English by Cranmer and Coverdale which, together with its uncompromising rubrics, established in March 1549 the Church of England for what it truly is – *Cum privilegio ad imprimendum solum Edouardi Whitchurche*. The year 1999 also saw what was almost a point of triumph emanating through the last forty years of cumulative activity without Royal Prerogative – smashing and destroying all those principles of which the Church of England has been a bastion; in fact, an energetic and unimpeded attempt to reduce it to a mere sect. Political and Ecclesiastical plans were already in train to achieve this, made the more easy by the natural apathy of other denominations and the general public to whom political parties sang their carefully scripted songs. We were urged to prepare celebration of a spurious millennium. The fact that King Herod died in 4 BC and that therefore the Massacre of the Innocents, together with a scientifically recorded Comet and the saving of the Christ-child took place in 5 BC, were matters to be conveniently ignored.

I must express my gratitude first and foremost to those boys who were my choristers during my years at Ely, together with the gentlemen, both past and still present, who formed the lay clerk body of that choir. Without them I could never have found that depth of knowledge which has remained with me, ever green, throughout my life.

My thanks are also due in particular to those innumerable people who have given of their time in critical readings of various parts of my manuscript, frequently suggesting further expansion and elucidation. To them, and to all others who have either hoorayed or harangued, I am indebted for a motive power almost worthy of C.B. Collett's 'Castle' class locomotives which used to cover the 118 miles from Bristol to Paddington in a mere 100 minutes – simply as a matter of course! But especially to Mrs Elisabeth Howard the author wishes to express gratitude beyond compare, for her patient criticism, her invaluable suggestions and her unstinting advice in the formation of this book over such a protracted period of time.

Michael Howard
Groombridge, Sussex
Ash Wednesday, 2001

Chapter I

Inspiration

One may as well begin at the 14th Evening, with Psalm 74: 'But now they break down all the carvéd work thereof: with axes and hammers' – and by citing one of the later fulfilments of these words as reported in the *Inventarium Monumentorum Superstitionis* of 1556: 'Rood lofts and painted pictures pulled down, sold, defaced or burned; statues smashed; Mass books, with all the rest of such feigned fables and peltering Popish books, all destroyed.' In 1569, Queen Elizabeth and all her adherents were formally excommunicated by Pope Pius V, and the Monarch became Head of the Church in England.

In 1998 I had read in divers broadsheets of the same story, except that this time there is a change of cultural locale. Today it burgeons from Archbishop Runcie's blithe launching of the *Alternative Service Book* of 1980, together with those incredible and pathetic volumes entitled the *New English Bible*. Yet now, *mirabile dictu*, the present Archbishop, Dr Carey, with his entourage of some two thousand female 'priests', has actually been seeking intercommunion with the Church of Rome. With breath-taking magnanimity, he is prepared to gloss over the fact that to the Catholic the Mass is a Sacrifice, while to the Protestant the Service of Holy Communion is a Memorial. With shattering insouciance, he proposes that the 'axes and hammers', together with all the work of Tyndale, Coverdale and Cranmer, are to be forgotten. He would appear to be puzzled by Rome's independent stance and her doctrine that there is no such thing as a female 'priest'. And one is given to understand that it is only a matter of time before the Church of England is to boast her first female 'bishop'!

'But it is never out of season to protest against that coarse familiarity with sacred things which is buy on the lip, and idle in the heart.' Thus, Dickens in his final Preface to *Pickwick Papers*.[1] Or more succinctly, 'All feelings and no doctrine', as the Reverend Peter Mullen entitles his contributory essay in the collection *Faking It*.[2] Nevertheless, while there are people without number who are staunchly against the attempt to introduce female 'priests' on the one hand, and equally a band of those who set out to preserve the traditional cathedral choir with its boys and men, both movements must be doomed to ultimate failure in that all their efforts are totally diversified. For there are those who are vociferously against female 'priests', but have not the slightest concern in the matter of cathedral choristers; and, of course, vice versa. Nor do either party make particularly clear upon what their preservations are to be liturgically based. Surely not the *Alternative Service Book* and the *New English Bible* – the latter a title meaningless in itself. Furthermore, there now looms an entirely new liturgy to be called 'Common Worship', of which, according to Dr Stancliffe, Bishop of Salisbury, we have already had a foretaste in the funeral of Diana, Princess of Wales – which included a pop-song from Elton John, sung by him in Westminster Abbey.

I have been young and now am old – being well past my allotted span of threescore years and ten. From time to time during my life I have certainly seen the ungodly apparently flourishing like a green bay-tree. But in comparison with the situation which has been brought about today, such incidents were but whimpers in the dark. I refer of course to that gradual but insidious erosion of the Church of England as it has manifested itself since 1980. Of its recovery from corruption to its true self during the course of the nineteenth century, there is no better nor more scholarly a guide than that presented by the Reverend Philip Barrett in his book *Barchester*, published in 1993 by the SPCK. To a Church still continuing in this recovery I was born in the September of 1922. So to vindicate my ingrained concerns in the whole matter, I hope without tedium, it becomes necessary for me to write in an autobiographical manner. I require to explain where I came from, how I was formed, where I went to, and from where I now view the whole subject in retrospect.

My paternal great-grandfather was a Master Tailor living in Ripley in Derbyshire. He must have been sensitive to the fine arts in general, for his eldest son, Frank Henry Howard, was a violinist and made violins. Indeed, in Poidras' *Dictionary of Violin Makers*, he is listed as having created some two hundred violins and eight or so violincelli.

His son, my father, and also named Frank Henry, obviously had his initial fiddle lessons from him, and was then sent to study at Miss Stockwin's Academy of Music in Nottingham. Such was the potential shown by him that Miss Stockwin persuaded Jesse Boot, of Boots the Chemists, to finance his moving to London and there to attend the Royal Academy of Music. By the age of twenty, he had become leader of Mr Henry Wood's Queen's Hall Orchestra, and his future appeared to be set.

I do not know at what point it was that he relinquished the violin in favour of the viola. What I do know is that he became a foundation principal in Beecham's Philharmonic and viola in André Mangeot's International String Quartet, of which Christopher Isherwood was the secretary. Alas, my father died in the November of 1934, killed by peritonitis. I was just twelve years old; he was thirty-nine.

To turn to the distaff side, my mother Florence was a noted watercolour artist. A small amount of her work, which escaped the exhibition sales, now hangs on my walls. It was once greatly admired by John Piper. Her eldest sister Nora was Director of Music at Bedford High School for Girls. Thus the scene became set for music and the arts in every sense. As a small child, I sat enthralled listening to my father practise and the Quartet rehearsing, sometimes finding myself inexplicably reduced to tears. I also regularly attended the Robert Meyer Children's Concerts at the Central Hall, Westminster. These programmes were always ably introduced and illustrated at the piano by the then young Dr Malcolm Sargent. On Sundays, my aunt would take me to Evensong either at Westminster Abbey (Ernest Bullock), St Paul's (Stanley Marchant), or Southwark Cathedral (E.T. Cook). I became overwhelmed with an unshakeable conviction that the time would come when I myself would be a cathedral organist.

We lived in the town of Ealing, some ten miles west of Marble Arch. Our house, enormous to my childhood memory, backed onto Walpole Park where, every year, charitable fairs with their steam traction engines, steam driven roundabouts, and all the cacophony of their wonderful mechanical organs utterly enthralled me. Ealing still had its own theatre, trams clattered their way down the Uxbridge Road, the Town Hall had its Grand Organ. Ealing Broadway Station served the Great Western Railway locally between Paddington and Maidenhead, while the main line carried luxurious express traffic – frequently headed by one of Collett's new Castle class – roaring magnificently and terrifyingly on its way, bound for the West country. My private school involved the road over this line, resulting in my frequent late arrivals – never to be cured by the savage beatings which were the price I paid.

There was also the small and rather basic bungalow on the end of the Romney Marsh as it terminated below the ancient town of Winchelsea. This was my mother's escape, and this was where I would go summer evening after summer evening with the local shepherd and his collie bitch, to watch as the flocks of sheep were rounded up, separated, examined, and tended. Often, on his arrival, he told me to use his signal to set the bitch off on her duties. As often, she would ignore me completely! As I grew older, I would walk for miles alone over the marsh, ever haunted by dreams of 'the cathedral' of which I must one day become the organist.

Meanwhile by my seventh birthday it was decided that I ought to have some preliminary grounding for the more formal education that was to come. On this basis I was sent (mornings only) to a nearby Dame's school – Winton House – a mere four or five minutes' walk from where we lived, and run by a Miss Storey of faintly repellant aspect. Basic numerical and alphabetical matters were, to me, of no great revelation. My aunt Nora had been supervising my piano and general musical education since my fourth year and these things, of course, took their natural place in such matters. Miss Storey and her staff spiced their general basic academics by reading to us children's stories, all of which seemed to take as their main point of departure calculated and unspeakable cruelty to animals. I remember, during one such, a small girl breaking down in uncontrollable floods of tears . . . and so the story was changed to something a little milder.

Girls, or boys, as companions I thought they were all pretty revolting. But there was one unanswered question – this business of *vive la différence*. So I enticed little Susan into a shady part of the garden and proceeded to take down her knickers. Her cries of distress speedily brought the matter to public notice – poor little Susan was only four years old. Rapidly I found myself faced by Miss Storey who told me that I was filthy, dirty, disgusting, utterly indecent, and that (reaching for the telephone) I was EXPELLED! The matter was never mentioned at home but I would guess that it provided my parents with some quiet amusement behind my back. Anyway, I was due for a short sharp shock when I got to my private school.

A year passed by and I was doing pretty badly in all subjects with the exception of scripture. I remember inwardly groaning with the thought that, like it or not, I would have to be a clergyman. As to French, all I could recall was the grisly tale of *Mandorf à la dent de fer*, and I think only that because *Mandorf* was a ghost. As to Latin, needless to say expounded by means of a primer assembled by some country clergyman, it was simply round and round the mulberry bush. Did country clergy have nothing better to do with their time than to torture small boys? After my first year concluded, my aunt Nora decided that a holiday on the other side of the Channel would do me good.

We took the boat train from Victoria for the Folkestone-Boulogne crossing. The ship that was to ferry us was the Southern's newly built *Maid of Kent* (1925), representing in all respects a scaled down and single smoke-stacked Atlantic liner. Alas, she gave her life in the course of evacuations from Dunkirk. Upon arrival at Boulogne we were treated to a break-neck (and to my mind now 'the wrong side of the road') auto-bus drive to the small town of Ambleteuse, where my aunt had engaged rooms at the hotel. I thought the food was delicious and I loved *la bonne* who waited upon us at table. Sadly, she spoke not a word of English and, apart from *la plume de ma tante* and such of that ilk, I had no French. I could not even tell her about *Mandorf*!

The town of Ambleteuse was virtually no more than a very large village, but was in no way exceptional in being graced by a magnificent Gothic church. I was allowed to be fascinated by its exterior, but my aunt said that on no account were we to go inside because it was Roman Catholic. Of course, this merely whetted my appetite and sneaking off one day I duly made my way within. The building was deserted, over my head flew stone vaulting, my footsteps echoed, and encased across the west wall was what was obviously the *Grand Orgue*. Facing east were sconces with innumerable little candles burning, a wonderful altar with six great candle sticks, a strange cowled housing in the centre (the Tabernacle), and ascending over all else a great Crucifix. The air carried a slightly stale but faintly sweet muskiness. Why was I supposed not to be there? If this was a manifestation of Heaven on Earth, surely it could not be wrong for me to be enjoying it? But it remained my secret. I never told my aunt.

We went to Cap Griz Nez to wish good luck to two highly greased swimmers who would be attempting the crossing on the next tide. We went to Boulogne with its superb Roman Road, but *not* to the Cathedral where Guilmant had once been Organist before proceeding to a similar appointment at *La Trinité* in Paris. We spent much time on the coastal sand dunes where I was relieved to meet a few other English children. I was sickened one day when passing the town butcher's shop to see a pig heartlessly slung across a wooden table, its throat slit from ear to ear. My aunt's perpetual state of high nerves was a constant irritation to me. Yet who can blame her – she a maiden lady and I an 'about to be' nine-year-old boy?

The time duly came for us to return to England and to be met at Victoria by my father with his Fiat motor car. But I have never forgotten that, the first of my only two *holidays* in France ... in a world that has now passed away for ever. It was the world of Michael Arlen: of the twenties – gay, stylish, mannered, bitter-sweet; a fraught mixture of cynicism and sentiment. A world that Evelyn Waugh tried to perpetuate throughout the next decade, but sadly failed in that vast purple patch, *Brideshead Revisited*. The world of Edgar Wallace's *The Flying Fifty-five*, of P.G. Wodehouse and Jeeves and Blandings Castle.

Although I gained so much from my private school – a thorough grounding in Latin, a lifelong love of *The Pickwick Papers*, a respect for good English – I was in fact far too introverted to benefit from its reputation for scholarships to Westminster and St Paul's. Also the death of my father had raised a financial nightmare. All I know of this is that the provisions which he had made, as had so many other musicians of his generation, were misappropriated by the administrative solicitor: a man named Bennet, who contrived to abscond with the lot. He was never brought to justice.

It was at this point that my aunt Nora, who had already cared so assiduously for my development, put herself financially *in loco parentis*. I believe that she held extensive shares in the four great railways, though the fascination that the Great Western Railway held for me was completely beyond her comprehension. I was removed from my private school and sent for a year to an 'enlightened' co-ed institution in Wimbledon; then coached for a full scholarship to Ellesmere in Shropshire. The carrot held before me was that if I gained my scholarship, I would be allowed to learn the organ. I was scarcely what one would have described as scholarship material, but by some process of sheer bloody-mindedness I contrived to pass the necessary papers. This was in the summer of 1936.

The holiday period which followed was, for me, what may virtually be described as boyhood's end. Hearing the Poulet Quartet and Poulet himself with Frank Laffitte in César Franck's Violin Sonata, Piano Quintet and (his penultimate work) the String Quartet – hearing artists like my father, Lionel Tertis, Gregor Piatigorsky – all these things now had to give way. The Wigmore Hall, the Queen's Hall, Sadlers Wells Opera must be, for the foreseeable future, displaced by another and totally unpredictable life of hell and damnation. I knew nothing of the significance of puberty and, as it gradually and ever increasingly manifested itself, became driven to the extremes of introversion and depression. Only the mysterious and adamantine conviction that was forever with me – my future as a cathedral organist – enabled me to withstand the indescribable miseries of life as it now became.

In the mid-September of that last haunting holiday I became fourteen years of age. The preceding weeks passed all too quickly – the sheep, the shepherd and his collie, the everlasting sound of the sea, the groan of the great fog-horn from Dungeness lighthouse on a misty evening, the smell of dung and dykes, the smell of incense at Sunday Mass in Winchelsea's ancient church – and I found myself with my mother at Rye Station waiting for the Wainwright D class locomotive with its 'birdcage set' to take us to Ashford and the London express. Then the District Line Railway to carry us to Ealing Broadway Station.

Once home came the final packing of my trunk, all of which had been prepared for during the late summer. Everything was named and numbered according to the official list, including a rug. Why was the rug so important? Carter Patterson duly appeared and the trunk was taken away. Items of immediate need were put into a small suitcase which I was to take with me. I had been placed in Woodard House, and was to be met at Euston by a senior boy called Murray-Jones who was to look after me during the journey. As far as I can remember, through these last two or three days I just felt completely numb; neither excited nor curious, neither sad nor frightened; like a being facing the inevitability of death.

At Euston, I was too confused to notice the famous Euston Arch (now destroyed in their infinite wisdom by British Rail). The fact that my train left from Platform 13 was, to me, like a knell. Murray-Jones was pleasant enough and courteous to my mother. The rolling stock was well appointed and comfortable. But I despised all the feverish bustle and noise. At Paddington, a Castle or a Manor would slowly back down, simmering and silent, to be coupled to its train. It would depart in the same way – no whistling, no explosive exhaust beats, given a little assistance from the rear by an uncoupled Pannier Tank until it was well clear of the platform.

But at Euston, departure was reduced to the level of a vulgar event. The locomotive's safety valves would be tearing the atmosphere to shreds: guard and station staff would be shouting, blowing whistles and waving flags; then, with a tremendous shriek, the self-important overblown locomotive would emit its first tremendous beats of exhaust, like the explosions of so many bombs. One would be tempted to think that there had never before been an express departure from Euston, on that or any other day. Either they just did not know how to do it, or they simply were not gentlemen! However, my contempt perhaps served, if only for a few moments, to take my thoughts away from my own troubles.

(Later in life I came to understand some illuminating facts. If the Great Western jealously preserved certain characteristics in its *modus operandi*, this was enough for the LMS to carry out its procedures in precisely the opposite manner. Meanwhile, at Exeter, where the Southern's famous *Atlantic Coast Express* had to cross the Great Western's road and share a station, the GW would do all that lay in its power to obstruct and delay the Southern's flagship train. Nevertheless, it must never be forgotten that all top-link drivers were, in their own right, just as great artists as were the organists who could decently and in good taste run the music of an English cathedral.)

I asked Murray-Jones what our housemaster was like. All that I knew of him was that his name was Hall. M-J appeared abstracted for a few moments. Then he said: 'Oh well, you know, he's quite a decent chap really.' Clearly, he was reluctant to pursue the subject. As a matter of fact, I was soon to find out everything about P.A. Hall. A Cambridge graduate, he was senior English master, and his encyclopaedic knowledge of decent English literature, both prose and verse, was devastating. This was balanced by his musical enthusiasms, and it was in his room that I was one night permitted to stay up and make my first acquaintance, through broadcast, with Bach's B minor Mass. On the other hand, he was a dangerously unpredictable character and possessed of a lacerating wit. He was also a hopeless drunkard and, on many occasions, had to be put to bed by the house-prefects. Eventually he was taken away – one presumes to some sort of home – to re-emerge after the war on the staff of a school in Harpenden. Sadly, for the man had genius, he failed to appear one morning and upon discovery was found to be dead.

The Euston express proceeded on its northern journey bound for Crewe (where we were to change trains) and ultimately to Liverpool. Indeed, Crewe with its great locomotive plant was to the LMS what Swindon was to the GWR. But whereas the west country expresses and the famous *Cheltenham Flyer* would go from Paddington to Swindon like bats out of hell, Euston to Crewe appeared to be a very erratic business, and the LMS had an overall and unenviable record for bad timekeeping.

At Crewe we disembarked and were joined by more boys who had travelled in from Liverpool, Manchester, and various surrounding places. I recall one boy in particular, heavily wrapped in an enormous great coat and shivering painfully with cold. He had come from South Africa. We were told that our next train would leave from a bay-platform on the west side of the station and that it would take us as far as Whitchurch. In a sense this seemed to me to be an additional cause for depression. The organist of Whitchurch Parish Church had once been a certain Edward German Jones and, as Edward German, he had composed a number of distinctly sub-Gilbert and Sullivan Operettas. Mercifully, his work is now almost forgotten.

But on turning to the bay-platform I suddenly experienced a consoling shot of relief. There before me stood a rake of four chocolate and cream Great Western coaches, and at their head, quietly simmering, a Great Western 2-6-2 Prairie Tank. Perhaps, to some, a mere straw in the wind; but to me, at that moment, several tons of superbly engineered comfort.

At Whitchurch we were joined by even more boys, and Shropshire and Welsh accents began to become apparent. Our next train was a GW Pannier Tank controlled auto-train: in other words, by a process of connecting controls from the locomotive, it could be driven from either end, the fireman remaining in the engine cab. This took us to Ellesmere Station itself, from which we set out through the by now failing light upon the long tramp into the country and to the College itself. From now on the meagre town of Ellesmere was out of bounds, and the Station

Master had strict instructions to impede and report any boy who might be foolish enough to attempt to abscond. Murray-Jones seemed, by this time, to have become absorbed into his own set, and those of us who were 'new bugs' simply followed the rest like so many lambs being led to the slaughter. A turn to the right, between two small hills, brought me face to face with the College and its main entrance complete with turret bell-tower. The shock was greater than anything I could possibly have anticipated. True, the school brochure had said that boys and masters all lived together under one roof – a fact common to all Woodard Schools at that time – but what I was now facing seemed to be no more than the sheer embodiment of a prison. A few cars of wealthy local farmers were drawing up at the main doorway, delivering their family offspring. A tall and painfully thin clergyman in a dark blue suit stood looking at us arrivals, just about as lost as so many of us felt at that moment. He was the new Chaplain, a Kelham-trained priest, and one who was to become to me a wonderful friend.

At this point my memories become somewhat confused. A Woodard House minion collected those of us 'new bugs' as were his concern, and taking us into the building, explained that the turret staircase might only be used by masters and gowned prefects and by no one else, except under 'fire' instructions from a senior. We were conducted along a cold cloisteral arcade from one side of which opened several doors: that to the Chaplain's study, that to the sitting and teaching room of the Director of Music, those to the general study for the gowned prefects and to the study of the Captain of School. We were to make use of a dangerously worn stone staircase at the end of the cloister, and by it were taken to our two House dormitories on the first level – one, Senior, one Junior. A typed notice indicated which beds had been allocated to each one of us. I and my new colleagues were, of course, at the bottom.

Beds! Crossed struts on an iron frame, two square horsehair 'biscuits', a flock mattress, coarse sheets and pillow case, two blankets and a thin bedspread. Now I realised where the rug came in!

At one end of the dormitory was a wooden screen shielding some six or eight wash basins with cold water taps only and mirrors above. Beside each bed was a cubicle to house one's immediate needs for daily toilet. The lavatories or 'bogs', as they were called, were open-ended stone latrines outside the rear of the main buildings. These we would be shown in due course. The two lavatories at the head of the turret staircase were for the use of our housemaster and for prefects respectively, except in cases of dire nocturnal emergency. If we presumed to 'give buck' to our seniors, we would 'pay for it in dorm before lights out'. We were directed to the dining hall to get a cup of tea and a couple of biscuits.

During tea, the Director of Music came round the new boys' tables
in order to take the names of those who were intending to take piano
lessons, and also to seek for any unbroken voices that might be of use,
either as trebles or altos, in the chapel choir (always a difficult problem
when the starting age can only be late thirteen to fourteen). I, of course,
willingly volunteered and was asked to see him for a voice trial the next
day. But when he heard that I wished to start learning the organ, it was
a very different matter. 'It is *not* a musical instrument,' he moaned.
'There is no point to it, unless you are interested in overcoming mechanical difficulties. However, we will talk about it tomorrow.' Once again,
that day, the sledgehammer of discouragement came down upon me. I
was no longer numb. I was plunging downwards and becoming more
and more lost; also, very frightened.

Yet, in retrospect, he must have known then that which I know now
and have known for many years: that among Woodard Schools alone
Alexander Brent-Smith, formerly an assistant organist to Sir Ivor Atkins
at Worcester Cathedral, had become a brilliant Director of Music at
Lancing College, numbering among his pupils of the time that great
artist Peter Pears; that H.A. Hawkins, a pupil of Widor, was the
Director at Hurstpierpoint and had the whole school singing plainsong
– that he shortly afterwards became Organist of Chichester Cathedral;
that Henry Coleman, a former Denstone College boy, was appointed
Organist of Peterborough Cathedral in 1921. Surely he must have
known! He had previously been Assistant Music Master at Denstone.
But I was ill-equipped, a young boy dealing with a dangerous and embit-
tered man of whom I shall have more to say later.

Utterly exhausted, in due course I followed the herd to evening
Chapel. There I was a little soothed as I listened to the Chaplain reading
the beautiful English of some Prayer Book collects. But when the whole
school came to dragging its lugubrious way through some maudlin chant
to the Nunc Dimittis, something deep within me fractured, and, with
lowered head, I shed floods of tears. Tears not for my mother nor for
my home; not for the Romney Marsh nor for the Great Western
Railway; not for Westminster Abbey nor for anything indeed for which
I could account; tears as from the depths of some divine despair; tears,
in fact, of uninhibited and revolting self-pity.

Chapter II

Inspiration Under Duress

Faintly, from some distant point, came the sound of a hand-bell ringing. I stirred uneasily, turning onto my back. The sound of the bell became more distinct and raucous. Opening my eyes, I was disconcerted to see a high ceiling above me that stretched away to both right and left. Opposite, a large uncurtained window. The sound of the hand-bell became shattering and then began to fade. It was seven o'clock and a watery sun shone without enthusiasm. 'Get up, you Squits,' shouted the dormitory captain (who was, in fact, Murray-Jones' younger brother). 'Get yourselves washed and dressed and don't waste time. Breakfast in Hall at eight sharp.'

Indeed I must have slept the sleep of utter exhaustion, for there was a sudden and sharp new awareness to everything that I would have preferred to do without; but also a feeling of some badly needed restored energy. The cold water, the cold linoleum underfoot, and the pushing of other boys ensured that one wasted no time over one's ablutions; one was soon downstairs and, to get off the stone flooring of the cloister and a vast ante-hall, I simply followed other equally bemused boys into Big School with its parquet flooring. (Of course the following did not register at the time, but it should be mentioned that Ellesmere Big School is most properly singled out in appropriate literature on nineteenth-century architecture, being of the vast length of ten stone bays surmounted by a breath-taking hammer-beam roof.) Here we pointlessly hung about until, summoned by the turret bell, it was time to go to the dining hall for breakfast. Little did we know that in the future there would be no such surplus time on our hands, and that every minute of every day would be carefully filled with some form of occupation, relevant or otherwise. It is true that we were never at any time required to stitch mail-bags, but the technique did underline the perhaps useful fact that 'anyone who has been to an English public school will always feel comparatively at home in prison.'[3]

Breakfast was alternatively porridge or cereal with milk of a strangely blue appearance. Obviously, it had been watered. This would be followed by a boiled egg, invariably hard, or bacon, usually charred. There was as much bread with butter/margarine mix as one cared to eat, with or without marmalade from which the taste of orange was curiously absent. Jugs of tea, tepid, completed this feast. On entry to the dining hall we stood in silence while Grace was pronounced from High Table: 'Benedictus benedicat per Jesum Christum Dominum nostrum.' Talking was then permitted while the 'skivs' pushed round trolleys collecting used plates. These same village girls would later go to make our beds. At all times were we forbidden to speak to them, and they used a separate back staircase from which we were banned. Prefects and house prefects sat at the heads of each table to see that all was kept in order. Staff ate at High Table with the Headmaster and his wife, and the food there was of a very different calibre.

The Head was the only married member of staff, and lived in a pleasant house with its own garden to the south of Big School. He also had his own study with internal telephone connection, off ante-chapel at the north end of the cloister passage. Next to him came the Secretary's room and then that of the Matron; finally, facing the main entrance and turret stair, the Army Sergeant, who also looked after the telephone switchboard and was encumbered with various other duties, ably assisted by the vile lout who rang that ghastly hand-bell each morning.

To return to the conclusion of this first breakfast, Grace was pronounced from High Table promptly at half-past eight. We stood while members of staff left, and were then dismissed in strict order of seniority, House by House. We had from then until the turret bell rang at 8.55 a.m., announcing Morning Chapel, to make our way through the dining hall crypt and the changing rooms out into the open air and to the 'bogs'. These latter were a series of hard floored, stone-walled and ceilinged cubicles with no doors, a lavatory pan with no seat, and toilet rolls apparently made out of some sort of fined down sandpaper. There was no privacy whatsoever. It behoved each boy to be as quick as possible so as to make way for the next in the queue. As far as I was concerned, a ready-made system for promoting constipation if ever there was one. Somehow, God knows how, I would have to find a solution to this revolting problem.

Morning Chapel differed from the evenings in that there was a psalm instead of a canticle and a lesson from the King James Bible, read by a gowned prefect. The Chaplain read the appropriate Prayer Book collects and other prayers, terminating in the Grace, and the service concluded with the hearty but leaden massacre of a hymn. Before and after the service, the Director of Music displayed a total lack of ability in the fine art of improvisation, simply meandering drearily from chord to chord to cover our entrance and exit. I had noticed that all the masters were either Oxford or Cambridge graduates, and wondered what could have been their private thoughts about all this, unless they were merely musically illiterate and non-receptive. The Director of Music himself was of neither the dark nor light blue universities, but a Bachelor of Music of Durham (degree taken externally). He was also the only member of staff who was *not* a gentleman.

The entire school had been ordered, on this first morning, to assemble after prayers in Big School, where we would be addressed first by the Headmaster and then by the Captain of School. Of the Headmaster's speech nothing registered except its undertones of dispassionate severity. But of the man himself I could now form a clear picture. An ebullient, black-suited, black-gowned clergyman, he was of vast and ponderous stature – always referred to throughout the school as either 'Ox' or 'Beef'. His speaking voice was utterly *profundo*, but totally unmusical. I suppose that, in common with so many headmasters of his ilk and generation, he secretly hoped that one day he might become a bishop. He never did.

Descending from the dais, he handed proceedings over to the purple-gowned Captain of School. Here my memories are sharply reawakened, for much of what this savage-voiced prefect had to say directly concerned me and the likes of me – and I did not much care for what I heard.

I learned that towards the end of the previous term a regrettable malaise had been pervading the school. This had got to stop and, furthermore, it was going to stop at once. Assiduous attendance would be expected at pre-breakfast open-air drill – sweat shirts and running shorts. Mid-morning break could be used for visiting the tuck shop, queuing in an orderly manner in order of seniority. Only prefects were allowed to make direct approach to the counter and their service would take precedence over all others. There must be no running at any time within the school buildings and all except prefects were forbidden to put their hands in their pockets. In any spare time, there must be no lounging about; each House had its own Day Room for relaxation. All inter-house rugby matches and all school matches must be attended on the touch line by those not playing, and suitable encouragement given to one's own side. To be excused from drill or games would require the production of an authorisation signed by the Matron. The bathrooms were out of bounds except once a week on the allocated House bath-night. Dormitories were out of bounds during the day. Washing facilities (a basin with cold water tap and a roller towel changed weekly!) could be found outside the door of the tuck shop. Shoes were to be changed daily for leather slippers before evening Chapel. Care must be taken to read all notices appearing on the boards in ante-Big School. No talking was permitted at any time in the cloister passages. Scrupulous attention to all this would gradually bring about some revival of the Public School Spirit in which Ellesmere was in danger of growing slack. Any deviations from these instructions would be treated with the utmost severity. 'I am giving the new boys a fortnight to settle in,' concluded the School Captain. 'After that, they will be treated the same as everyone else. New Boys will now go to their House Day Rooms.'

Our Day Room was nothing to enthuse about in itself: two or three badly worn basket chairs and some upright chairs; a quarter-size billiard table; some shelves with a motley collection of mangled books; waste baskets full of the papers torn from tuck shop purchases. But the view on a fine summer's day must have been breath-taking, facing west, as it did, to the Welsh hills.

House prefects were in evidence, and one by one we were button-holed for a talk. This created an atmosphere pertaining to something important, and ultimately, for me as it turned out, to be of grave importance. But the discussion as such was very much on one side. What it amounted to was 'Did I wish to join the Boy Scouts or the Officers Training Corps?' The Scouts, as its name implied, was really for boys as such, and they just played games. The OTC however was a serious matter, and meant that in the event of war I could gain a commission and lead my men into battle (being, amongst other things, among the first to meet a speedy death – but that bit was left out!). Cornered like this, there could really be only one answer, and I was told that I would be duly issued with the full uniform of a private, plus my own rifle and a bayonet. Voila! – *dans la piège*; and how easily it was done!

Finding that there was still some time to go before luncheon (or was it dinner?), I made my way to the Director of Music's room to be appraised for the chapel choir and to arrange about having organ lessons. My top notes were beginning to go, but I hoped that I might sing on the alto line. A snag to this was that I must stand in the front row with the trebles because, for my first year, I had to wear an Eton collar with my black suit. So I must for the time being do the best that I could as a pseudo-treble. But, as an organ student, would it not be better that I should be in the organ loft with him? He would see what could be arranged. As to an eventual organ scholarship to King's College, Cambridge, or to the Royal Academy in London, one had to be absolutely brilliant to have any hope whatsoever; and my dreams of a cathedral . . . I might as well forget them. Again, feeling utterly forlorn and obviously showing it, I was shattered suddenly to find myself in his arms. With a lurching push I sent him staggering back, and from then on everything was absolutely business only. In a way he was blackmailed, for I had only to report the incident for him to have found himself and his suitcase proceeding briskly on the road to Ellesmere Station.

Norman Frederick Byng Johnson (known throughout the school as 'Bung') was a sordid and pathetic mess. He was equally incapable of training either the individual voice or a choir. His twice-weekly practice for trebles simply consisted in the meaningless rehearsing by rote of whatever he had chosen to put down on the music list. His full practices, once a week in chapel, were a shambles. There was no ensemble, nor was there any instruction on how to achieve it. Boys, including prefects, sang in the choir because it was a school of ecclesiastical temper, and because they would have been genuinely grateful for some musical instruction. Meanwhile the colossal drag of sound from the full school ruined everything, and was carried on with complete disregard to any lead from the organ. A congregational practice was unheard of. Mercifully, hymns were chosen by the Chaplain and the Headmaster.

Evensong on Saturdays and Sundays were fully choral with settings of the canticles and an anthem. The Sunday Eucharist, decently celebrated by fully robed priest with altar boy, severs and altar candles, was subjected to appalling musical settings such as Berthold Tours in C, Eyre in E flat, and similar bathos. Only the Creed was sung to Merbecke, and then to Stainer's lame and lumpish version of the original. The best we got to at Evensong was Arnold in A and Stanford in B flat; from there it was downhill fast to Bunnett in F and Byng Johnson in E flat. No music was ever sung unaccompanied. Unexpectedly, out of a selection of anthem-trash, we sang Brahms' *How lovely are thy dwellings fair*. It would have been kinder not to have done so.

To conclude these opening days, we were called to the surgery for dental inspection. I was passed 'fit', as I knew I would be; but I thought that the dentist, who travelled in from Oswestry, seemed a decent and likeable person. Not so the MO – a chinless wonder who inspired no confidence whatsoever. For him we were lined up to receive our anti-flu injections. One by one we were impersonally stabbed in the flesh of the upper arm, to be pumped full of some serum that made one feel terrible for the next forty-eight hours. For each one of us, the same syringe, the same needle. As to hygiene, you just took your chance with the rest. Happy days!

When Sunday afternoon came, orders were that we must get out of the building and walk. The undeviating road encircling the College must have run to at least two miles. Knowing nobody in particular, I set off on my own without purpose or enthusiasm through strange and seemingly drab country – hedges, fields, cows, mud: mud, fields, cows, hedges. The Headmaster drove by in his motor car, raising an impersonal hand. I doubt that he would have known who I was.

But a comforting solution was closer than I thought. When, on my second or third Sunday I returned, I found the Housemaster of Talbot House standing outside the turret gate – and with him a black and white coated spaniel. As I approached, he smiled and said, 'Well, namesake, how are you getting on?' – for his name too was Howard. Politely, but with restrained urgency, I asked *please* might I be allowed to take his dog with me on my Sunday walk, providing that at all times I kept him on the lead. His reaction was that it would probably do us both good, and from then on I was always assured of a companion on those dreary afternoons. I had, at last, stumbled across some humanity. Howard of Talbot House even confessed to musical interests but, as always, the subject of College music was carefully avoided.

Gradually the term lumbered its way into winter. There was no effective warmth except in masters' studies and those of gowned prefects, where coal fires would blaze cheerfully. The usual irritations of youth beset us – styes, pink eye, chapped and cracked hands, chilblains. A particular horror was impetigo, when one had to wear a mask upon one's face. No one seemed to think of improving the sanitary arrangements, such as replacing more regularly that filthy towel that hung outside the tuck shop.

Daylight degenerated into a sombre grey; but the end of term was approaching, with its farce of a candle-lit carol service in the chapel. Suddenly anxiety struck. There was an outbreak of mumps. Would one get home for Christmas or have to remain imprisoned in the sanatorium? I was among the lucky ones, and on a dark and freezing morning joined the long trek back to Ellesmere Station and to eventual civilisation. Those who lived close enough to be collected by car had already left after tea on the previous day.

Chapter III

Inspiration Burgeons

Ellesmere, Whitchurch, Crewe, and the Euston express which invariably arrived late at its London destination. Here I would be met by my mother, and we then travelled back by Inner Circle and the District Railway to Ealing Broadway. Asked if I had had a good term, I knew that going into the truth would be met with no sympathy. 'All young boys think it the thing to moan about school upon arriving home for the holidays.' I responded with selectively negative information and left the matter there. After all, as Pilate said: 'What is truth?' But I could not disguise the fact that I was desperately in need of a decent meal; in fact, many of them.

It was virtually with surprise that I discovered that the world of comparative freedom really did exist. Warmth and a comfortable bed. Freedom to come and go. Walpole Park. Trams. Shops. The Great Western Railway. St Pauls and Westminster Abbey – not only on Sundays, but also on weekdays if I wished, for I was now considered old enough to get about by myself. It was as if that other world of Ellesmere was but an horrible dream, and Christmas was approaching. Furthermore, arrangements were made for me to practise the organ in a local church.

I mainly frequented Westminster Abbey where weekday Evensong was sung at 3 o'clock in the afternoon. Visually I admired the Royal Charter Red cassocks and Gothic surplices of the choristers and lay-vicars, and was overwhelmed by the stately way in which everything was conducted in this glorious vaulted church. The organ, divided on the pulpitum (or screen), was the old Hill instrument which was, by now, mechanically dilapidated and, sadly, never to be restored. The standard of singing reflected Ernest Bullock's stern sense of efficiency, and the music sung was either Tudor, Restoration, or faceless contemporary with some leavening of better Victoriana (though it was here that I first heard Wood's beautiful Evening Canticles in C minor). I used to walk through the screen arch in good time and, being male, get one of the vergers to lead me to an unoccupied canopied stall to east or west of the choir stalls themselves. In due course, I got Dr Bullock to allow me to sit with him on the screen in the centre of which was the organ console. It was then that I realised what an absolute over-strung mass of nerves this frightening man was – thus accounting for all the abruptness of manner and rigidity of principles. Poor man, he had been badly shell-shocked while serving in France as captain and adjutant during the Great War and, as if that were not to be enough, his home, belongings and papers were all destroyed during the Second World War when in 1940 a bomb found his house in Abbey Little Cloister.

Unfortunately, his problems were detrimental to his choristers. While always correct, their tone lacked centre and was somewhat breathy. They all regarded him with some degree of fear. He was narrow and lacked a sense of fun, and they infinitely preferred his assistant organist, Dr Osborne Peasgood. (I reached all these conclusions over a period of time – hardly during my first holiday from Ellesmere!)

So passed in fulfilled happiness the days up to Christmas and the New Year of 1937. Then the horizon began to darken as the time started to draw uncomfortably close to my returning to Ellesmere. But one morning I woke up to find my jaws and my glands in excruciating agony. The greatest gift had befallen me, for I had contracted mumps! The doctor was called and said I must be confined to my room, and that a fire should be lit. He gave various other instructions and said that he would return from time to time. On no account must I be moved. Eating – soup, eggs and the like may have been torture, but, as we learned to say during the war: 'Who cares with duck on the menu!' And my aunt Nora bought me a book – Batsford and Fry's recently published *English Cathedrals*.

I am not, and never have been, prone to superstition. Yet over and over again in my life have I become conscious of the workings of a power greater than myself. Carefully studying my way through that book I became strangely fixed with the chapter and photographs of Ely. One of these latter, taken from the south-east bank of the river Ouse, showed the cathedral riding like a great ship over the tiny city of some eight thousand inhabitants. Another, shot from under the Octagon, showed the magnificent Norman nave running back to the West Doors and Galilee, the nave itself surmounted by Gambier Parry's decorated wooden ceiling. A third showed the wooden screen and stone vaulted choir with, on the North side, the great Gilbert Scott organ case derived, to some extent, from that to be found at Strasburg. Ely seemed to haunt me and I vowed that sometime, as soon as possible, I must go there and see the place for myself . . .

Alas, all too soon this respite came to an end and I was pronounced

fit to return to school. So to Euston and to Platform 13 where stood
Michael Wiggins, gowned prefect and captain of my House. The same
fate, mumps, had befallen him. He was charming to my mother, said
how pleasant it would be to have a companion for the journey, and we
boarded the train. In no way did he make me feel junior to himself but
broke down my shyness with easy conversation, never dwelling on sport
which he knew was not my area and never alluding to musical matters
in which he knew that his knowledge was inferior to mine. In fact, he
was the perfect gentleman. We deplored the unpredictable timings of
the LMS, agreed that the GW was an infinitely superior line, bemoaned
the dreary tramp from Ellesmere Station to the College. But once there,
he made for his study while I lugged my suitcase up to the bottom
end of my freezing dormitory. I attempted to report my return to my
housemaster, but poor Hall appeared to be deeply and unshakeably
asleep. So downstairs miserably to tea.

Callow schoolboys never miss an opportunity – they would be abnor-
mal if they did. Everyone knew why I, in common with several others,
had been delayed in my return. Nevertheless I was treated as if, at their
expense, I had snatched a few jolly days in Paris. We all followed this
code, and those who did not accept it as a part of accepting life's inexplicable knocks, invariably had trouble with achieving so-called
maturity, sometimes leaving school and university as permanent misfits.
Woe betide parental indulgence. By degrees, I formed my own physical and psychological armour and it seldom failed me, either then or
later in adult life.

Clearly my life fell into two departments – the manageable and the,
perhaps, not so easily managed. There was the manageable department
of Byng Johnson and my organ tuition. He was quick enough to recognise exactly where he stood with me vis à vis myself and his
homosexuality. He also saw that as an organ student I was grimly determined and, in spite of his own revolting musical tastes, he turned out
to be a brilliant, one might say a compulsive, teacher from the technical standpoint. By the end of my first term I had acquired a fluent
pedalboard technique, and was now going through the drill of combin-
ing this with an independent manual technique. I was expected to
practise arduously three times a week, and this arrangement in itself
freed me from many irritations such as the endless touch-line support-
ing of rugby matches and (frequently) being trampled upon and caked
with mud when actively involved with 'club-sides'.

Soon I was facing the Eight Short Preludes and Fugues attributed to
Bach, as well as being taught the arts of practical service accompaniment. All this made me vastly unpopular, but I lived more and more in
a world of my own. Sneering and dormitory ragging was but a small

price to pay, and eventually my peers and my seniors tired of the occupation. Other advantages began to manifest themselves, such as slipping off to the 'bogs' on my way to or from the organ loft; the use of a back wooden staircase to the organ loft itself; and being left in peace should I be studying a musical score during evening prep.

But one particular burden was combined with all this – to gain a degree in music, either at Cambridge or elsewhere, was essential. In those days there was no cathedral organist without this paper qualification – and most of them held doctorates. Hence, you might have sloppy playing, ragged and ill-trained choristers, a sadly limited musical horizon, but a pretty piece of academic dress was a *sine qua non*. This for me meant Cambridge (the most enlightened) or London through the Royal Academy, and therefore it was imperative for me to end my Ellesmere days with Oxford and Cambridge University Entrance safely beneath my belt.

There is no doubt that the individual class teaching in those days preceding the war was of a particularly high standard. My namesake, Howard, whose subject was general history, conjured up fascinating pictures of political sequences and how they affected the arts of painting, architecture and music as they related to all that surrounded them. That Romanesque building became more delicate as it journeyed northwards – leading eventually to a new concept in France which we call Gothic, and which became as delicate and fragile in that country as it failed to do in Germany. I began to hear the musical parallels in my head. That in England, we had inherited the Romanesque vision through the Normans, but that its character in this country was highly individual. That the eventual English attempt at pure Gothic, now wantonly stripped of its various functional screens, seemed little better than a cold and vast ecclesiastical railway tunnel. That the great nineteenth-century architects of cathedral 'restoration' had often done as much harm as they had done good. That there were balancing concepts to be found in all other arts, which we could in time discover if we so wished. Byrd and Palestrina or Beethoven and Mozart; painters of English landscapes and horses, of Dutch interiors, of French countryside. Why? Why this diversity? Why was an Englishman emphatically not like his French or German counterpart – or indeed his Scottish and Welsh neighbour: (cries of 'Sir!' and groans from various boys named Jones. There were thirteen such in the school during my time).

Hall of course was an absolute inspiration on all manifestations of the English language, provided that he happened to be sufficiently sober to communicate. Otherwise he would lapse into a searing wit that frequently passed even our powers of comprehension. K.G. Todd brought Latin to life via Greek mythology (thereby killing two birds with one stone) and a manner of strident good-nature. 'Boy,' he would shout, 'you ought to be beaten like an egg!' – and 'Howard, was that you treadling the organ in chapel this morning? Yes? I thought you treadled it remarkably well!' So one came to realise that these men, while standing for no nonsense, were one's friends and quite unlike the masters of one's private school, to whom one was really no more than a money-earning form of nuisance: – Ante, apud, ad, adversus, Circum, circa, citra, cis; Contra, ergo, extra, infra, jingle, jangle, jingle, and a smart clip across the back of the head if one failed to get it right. Indeed Latin was a dead language! Not one of them thought to question what sort of an English language we might have had, were it not for its foundations and derivations.

Todd, as a classicist, would howl with pain if one presumed to split an infinitive or to end a sentence with a preposition. 'Go and look at Bosch's *Haywain*. From where does it come, and to where does it go? If you can't get to Madrid, any tawdry reproduction will at least teach you to use your eyes.' On and on he would fulminate about structure and proportion . . . 'and now have the grace to apply a little respect to Latin and to the language which is *supposed* to be native to you.' I thought of sonata form, the rondo, the anchorage of the passacaglia. And I have often wondered what became of that man. There was a war coming.

Back to Byng Johnson. With my gradual mastery and memorising of most of the Eight Short Preludes and Fugues something further must be found: and I suppose that I was lucky that it was nothing worse than the Six Sonatas by Mendelssohn. Of these, I started by working on No. 2 in C minor – perhaps the most cohesive of the so-called Sonatas that were really loosely constructed Suites.

In addition, I was required to play for at least one morning and one evening chapel service each week, and here 'Bung' left me entirely alone to do my own preparation. I do not think that he was ever truly able to accept that I was a 'serious' music student with a future mapped out in my own mind. If he did, he certainly never forgave me, sneering and pouring contempt whenever possible. In fact, my debt of gratitude to that man is beyond description . . . he set out to break me, and the result was precisely the opposite. I asked him to order for me vocal scores of Gibbons' Canticles in F and those by Purcell in B flat, having heard and been intrigued by both at Westminster Abbey. Bung's scorn was absolute: 'early gropings from ill-informed days'; but the scores duly arrived.

Father Sharp, the Chaplain, had duly sent for me. A pleasant room, a coal fire, comfortable chairs. He knew about my ambitions. Had I been confirmed? Was I prepared to attend confirmation classes? Did I realise that the duties and responsibilities of an organist were second only to those of the priesthood?

I ought to beware of some of the things I heard offered in the name of worship; after all, only the best was good enough for God. But, as always, no names were mentioned. It was simply a case of making sure that the donkey's nose was pointed in the right direction. What had my father done? What concerts and recitals had I been to? Why did I like Westminster Abbey? Did I know my Prayer Book thoroughly? If I had doubts or felt muddled, his door was always open to me. Meanwhile, he would put down my name to attend his classes in preparation for confirmation. I was duly confirmed by the Bishop of Lichfield.

Next, two things of importance happened: a new art master named Eric Waddams joined the staff, being freshly down from King's College, Cambridge, where he had been a choral scholar under that redoubtable musician Boris Ord. He sought and gained permission to form a Madrigal Society . . . and Byng Johnson announced (with considerable sourness) his intention to resign and, in fact, to retire. 'So you want to run with the hare and hunt with the hounds,' was one of his final and most viciously uttered remarks to me. I was not upset. Only a few days previously I had been urgently called from my bed and, clad in pyjamas and dressing gown, rushed to the organ loft to play Merbecke for an early Sung Eucharist celebrating some red-letter Saint's Day. With quiet amusement, I wondered with what irony 'Bung' would contrive to write my end of term report.

Eric Waddams' Madrigal Society proved to be for me an absolute and highly influential revelation. Not only did Waddams adopt what must have been the basics of Boris Ord's techniques in his training – we were all encouraged to sing with smooth line and clear words – but he made us aware that each voice part should be treated as a melody in its own right. Growling and half hooting voices became relaxed and musical in intent if not in fact under his supple direction. 'Play your "cello"', he would say with a sweep of his arm to the somewhat reach-me-down basses – and the lines of music gradually became interwoven.

Then there was the music itself. Much of it was from *The Triumphs of Oriana*, that wonderful collection of madrigals in praise of Queen Elizabeth. Each one of these pieces invariably ended with the same words: 'Long live fair Oriana' – as it were, like a secular *Gloria Patri*. Sadly, when in 1603 the complete set was published, Oriana was no more. Queen Elizabeth had died earlier that year.

Why, I wondered did these wonderful composers write only for the world of entertainment and flattery? Eric Waddams could soon have put me right on this point had I chosen to ask. But I didn't. Callow youth that I was, I was afraid of making a fool of myself. Furthermore, my ignorance was common amongst musicians and the general public. Here, in fact and unbeknown to myself, was one of the seeds which was later to burgeon into the Renaissance Society.

A boy called Spoonley was the most tremendous, if unconscious, aid to my maintaining a balanced sense of proportion. Feebly dabbing at a typewriter one afternoon in Big School, Spoonley rushed up to me shouting 'Howard – mind you don't overtake yourself!'. In anger, I found myself typing a lot of fraction signs instead of letters. On another occasion he approached me slowly, looking most sombre indeed. I asked him in all sympathy what the trouble might be. 'Well, Howard,' he responded lugubriously, 'you see, I haven't got a mother.' I said how dreadfully sorry I was and when had this happened. 'Oh' he answered, 'I never have had a mother.' Never had a mother? 'No – you see,' with shame of face, 'somebody played a dirty trick on my auntie.' For perhaps some thirty seconds I was appalled and then the penny dropped. So naturally I let him 'have it'. We were caught by a gowned prefect and were both soundly thrashed.

But before continuing the musical saga of my third and final year at Ellesmere, I must return to the other department of my life – the one that seemed, at least on the face of it, to be a not so easily managed proposition . . . I refer, of course, to that apparently unmitigated curse, the OTC. But here again, as if some guardian angel were looking after my best interests, an accident and the practice of some low cunning came temporarily and profitably to my rescue. The matter deserves its own chapter.

Chapter IV

Scherzo

Altogether there were three OTC parades each week. On Tuesday and Friday, morning school had a shortened 'break' and finished some twenty minutes earlier than on other days. This was to allow for a 'mufti' parade, involving only army belt, cap and rifle. But the parade on Tuesday afternoon was a full-dress affair for which one was supposed to have made preparation during Monday and the break after Tuesday's breakfast. Army boots polished like mirrors, belts perfectly blancoed, all brass buttons plus belt-buckle polished to absolute translucence; rifle cleaned, oiled, and properly 'pulled through'; bayonet and scabbard greased and cleaned. Any failures noted during parade inspection and one's name and number would be duly noted for 'extra parade'. 'Remember, in war, a man's best friend is his rifle!'

I could never get it right. There was always blanco on the buttons and, when removed, there would be brasso on the belt. The boots insisted on remaining a sulky dull and the leather round my cap was opaque. My 'best friend' seemed intent upon having a barrel like an underground railway tunnel; my bayonet just did not look fit to kill anyone without it appearing, in some way, to be a personal insult. Week after week the inspecting officer drew upon his sarcastic plenty and week after week my drill and turn out became more and more erratic. It was clear that there must be trouble, and big trouble, in the end, and from what I knew of army punishments, it all looked pretty bleak. Perhaps I *was* fourteen years old, but how I wished that I had joined the scouts. I applied to change; the application was refused.

My uniform was that of a Great War private, and to don it correctly in the available half an hour was a feat both marvellous and peculiar. Khaki trousers held by braces fastened below the knee. Boots, once *in situ* and laced, were then applied to with puttees which one wound around one's leg up to the trouser – too tightly and everything throbbed, a shade loose and they came adrift, thus landing one in further trouble. Khaki jacket buttoned to the neck and the belt correctly applied. Finally the cap, absolutely fore-square, no angling permitted. Then off to the armoury to collect one's 'best friend' and the bayonet. Now exhausted and hopeless to the parade ground and 'fall in'. Stand at ease; atten-SHUN; slope-HIPE; as you were . . . Slope-HIPE. Wait for it, as the officer and sergeant approach one's section.

On 11th November each year the whole lot of us were formed into a great platoon and marched, following the band, down the dreary road to Ellesmere Church – an ancient building uglified by much unfortunate 'restoration' and improvement. It was 1936 that saw my first experience of this charade. First, an incredible service with an organist who would have been, and probably was, better at ploughing a field; and the corps tearing to saccharine shreds such nauseous gems as 'O valiant hearts'. Then to the War Memorial: 'We will remember them.' Of course we must not pray for them. We were Protestants and they were dead.[4] A bugle blowing *The Last Post*. A town band attempting to play the National Anthem. Intuitively, I took off my cap. My God! . . . I was hauled up before the Commanding Officer when we returned. Another milestone in 'the happiest days of one's life'.

Something would have to be done, but for the life of me I could not think what. Then one day in my second year the miracle came about – but, like all miracles, apparently completely by accident.

It was a Tuesday. Midday meal was over, and there was the usual insane rush to be kitted out to as near perfection as possible before going on parade. I cannot remember what exactly it was, but something had happened which meant that, do what I would, I could not possibly get onto the parade ground on time – and to be late would mean dire punishment as laid down by army regulations. Nobody seemed to have any time to look at me or to notice where I was, so by a series of unhurried but subversive moves I made my way to the library which I knew would be deserted. From there, I heard all the usual sounds of a Tuesday uniform parade getting under way: the shouts of command, the stamping of feet, the drums and bugles of the band growing fainter – and then, silence. I dared to come from behind a vast bookcase and to sit down. There was, of course, the problem of what to do when parade ended, but it seemed that it would probably be best to stay where I was until the bell rang for tea. If anyone came in during that comparatively short final interval, I might just as well have done the same thing, so there would be nothing to arouse comment. I began to examine the books on the shelves.

I noted that the subject of music was conspicuous by its absence. No Groves. No *Oxford Companion*. Perhaps just a reflection of Bung's miserable attitude, for surely he would be among those who could make recommendations to the library authority. But other subjects were to a greater or lesser degree well represented, not least ecclesiastical architecture. The first things to catch my eye were two volumes published by, of all people, the Great Western Railway Company; one on English Cathedrals and one on English Abbeys. Then I spotted the Batsford and Fry book on Cathedrals, which I already possessed. Also, their publication on The English Abbey. Bradley-Birt's book on Tewkesbury and a book on the great 'wool' churches of Suffolk and Norfolk added further to my curiosity, and there were also illustrated books on Parkes Bonnington, Turner, and Constable. In fact, a veritable treasure trove stood before me, and one which I must somehow absorb until it became in truth mine own. There lay the problem.

First of all I looked carefully for any sign that I had been missed from corps parade. There appeared to be none. So far, so good. After all, where did one find any particular trace of individuality between one piece of cannon fodder and another? To assess an army, a company, a platoon, a section, on such a basis would be an impossibility. And my best plan would be to take advantage of the general post-luncheon mêlée and simply go straight to the library and close the door. I could not afford to sacrifice any of my allotted organ practice time, and this newly aroused interest was not only compulsive but also creative; not destructive, as was the whole basis of the OTC.

So this is the plan I followed, armed with notebooks which began to contain an evolution of English parish church architecture as I assembled it from Saxon times onwards; and from that mid-winter term, through the spring term, and until half way through the summer term I successfully led this double life. In the end, it was my 'best friend' that gave me away. An armoury inspection showed that his bore had grown what looked like a comfortable fur coat, while my bayonet blade had become opaque and rust encoated. I was sent for by the Commanding Officer.

The meeting was a 'mufti' occasion, but the CO was in no mood to make it any the less formidable for all that. Did I realise that the rifle and bayonet which I had so nearly ruined were not mine to treat in such a manner? They belonged to the War Office. My neglected uniform belonged to the War Office. I myself as a member of the OTC was ultimately answerable to the War Office. I was guilty of desertion and, in time of war, would undoubtedly have been shot. At this point I almost expected him to present me with a revolver and a bottle of whisky, saying, 'Well, I shall now leave the room for half an hour. In the meantime, you know what to do.'

Instead, I was told that I must restore my rifle and bayonet to their pristine glory, that the same thing applied to my bedraggled uniform, and that I should parade on the following Tuesday under Sergeant-

Major's supervision. In a final burst of infinite disgust, he asked me was I prepared to stand by while the Germans raped my sisters and their girl-friends? (I had no sisters.) I tried the one about our raping '*their* sisters and *their* girl-friends', but it was not well-received. A soldier trained by the OTC was also a 'gentleman'. I was dismissed to await further developments.

I conscientiously did all that I could for my 'best friend', though never restoring him quite to his first fine careless glory; and I also did my best for my bayonet. The rest of that weekend was taken up with brasso and blanco and dubbin, in some efforts to make my uniform fit to be seen in public. Then, on the Tuesday morning, the CO's orders for the day were posted on the usual notice board. For some they made for enter-taining reading.

Platoons and sections would assemble with rifles and bayonets in the usual way on the parade ground, as would the Band. All Officers and NCOs would be in full dress uniform. There would be a general inspec-tion followed by a Route March which, because of its length, would occupy the entire afternoon.

Added to all this information came another notice headed DESERTERS PARADE. The Deserter would fall in on the parade ground under the supervision of a Sergeant. He would be dressed in full uniform and carry a rifle with fixed bayonet at the slope arms position. He would also carry a pack upon his back in which would be placed three bricks. He would stand and/or march to attention at all times. Co-incidentally, it was a day of blazing heat in mid-June.

I suppose I thought, 'Damn them. If this is their way of getting at me, let them get on with it. There won't be any obstruction from me.' And that is precisely how it turned out to be. Even when the platoon was permitted to 'fall out' for a while in order to regain steam, my personal SM kept me at it: 'left-right-left-right-about-TURN; left-right-left-right-' and so on ad nauseam. I just became mindless, and by the time we returned to College, with the bugles and the drums blowing and clatter-ing, I kept it up until formally dismissed and then marched away.

That evening found me shivering beyond control, and I was sent to bed. In the night a fever set in and I eventually became aware that I was in the Sanatorium. I was not aware of feeling ill, uncomfortable, in pain, or anything else. All I wanted to do, and all I did, was sleep.

Then one morning, probably only some two or so days later, I became aware of a figure standing beside my bed. It was the Commanding Officer. In friendly manner he enquired how I was feeling, and told me that although I was still a private in the OTC, I would be excused parades for the rest of that term; but I must be prepared to do my best with whatever was asked of me when College reassembled in the autumn. If I would undertake this, then everything would be done to help me. (Seen in retrospect, it is clear that I had given them all a jolly good fright!) Other masters (but not Bung) came to seem me, and I was put on a diet that must have been comparable to that of High Table. Gradually my only desire was to get back into the organ loft and resurrect my playing. But I also gave Mr Howard my precious notebooks on church architecture and asked him to look through them. Back in school, there was no reference to my OTC saga, and my present release from parade duties. Mr Howard duly returned my jottings on English churches, together with some constructive suggestions and a five shilling postal order to put towards the next book that I might be buying on the subject.

Although with the arrival of the Christmas term my OTC respite was at an end, I found that in so far as it was possible I was involved in matters of very meagre demand. Ironically, it was this very policy which led, not to further trouble for me, but to a situation of acute embarrassment to the Senior Officers and, indeed, the Corps itself.

One Tuesday in mid-November had been set aside for a grand tactical scheme to be enacted on the hill and round the woodland situated on the north side of the College buildings, and a General or somebody similar was coming down from the War Office to inspect and pronounce on the whole thing. I, being regarded as of no brain even in elementary military matters, together with another boy of similar ilk, were to be given the 'safe' job of adding the appropriate scenic effects – simply, from our concealed point, of letting off a series of fireworks. On the relevant day, Harwood, for that was the name of my partner, and I were to await a carefully prearranged signal, and then to commence this simple operation. We were briefed time and time again until, surely, nothing could possibly go wrong.

On the great day itself, we lay in our concealment, wearing none too presentable uniforms and making use of a couple of waterproof capes. Before us stood an enormous box containing fireworks of every description. We had both been 'put in the picture'. 'A' company was to approach from the right; 'B' company from the left. Both companies would be armed with blank cartridges. It was upon their meeting face to face that we were supposed to provide the 'verisimilitude' that would cause the exercise to end in a planned 'shambles'. Elementary!

It was misty, there was a slight drizzle coming from the south-west, and we felt extremely cold. With pathetic consideration, Harwood attempted to give the fireworks some protection with a piece of sacking. We lay and shivered in silence in what appeared to be a time-deserted world. 'Oh for the warmth of a woman's body,' I thought with shamefully 'impure thoughts'. I had a lot to learn, and at Ellesmere musing on the opposite sex was regarded as the lowest form of 'smut'. Likewise, I believe that homosexuality was virtually absent. Bung was not a good advertisement. And when it came to the subject of the Abdication, we just did not know what everybody was carrying on about! Mrs Simpson looked to us to be an ugly old bitch. Surely one could do better than that.

Suddenly we became aware of voices and movement away to our right. 'I think it's begun,' said Harwood. 'No sounds from the other side,' I observed. 'Probably direction of the wind,' he said. 'Do you think we ought to start on the crackers?' I remarked that we had received no signal, and then we became aware that neither of us was at all sure what kind of a signal it was supposed to be anyway. Things were definitely going on. Perhaps we might send off one explosive and see what was the reaction.

Harwood picked out a particularly vicious looking sort of a blockbuster from the box, and I put a match to the fuse. At once it began to hiss and splutter in an extremely 'this means business' way. Hastily, Harwood dropped it – back into the box! The sound of over-frying bacon began to increase and then came the first explosion ... followed by another, and another, and another, each growing in enthusiastic intensity and suggesting, more and more, a *grand choeur* of happy destruction. Then the whole lot went up, blowing the box to smithereens and producing a huge and dense pall of suffocating smoke that began to drift away across the 'field of battle' ... followed by a strange and inexplicable silence.

A voice was heard shouting angrily, answered by others more distant and the sound of horses coughing. Horses? There should have been no horses. What on earth was going on? We crouched behind a clump of bushes and waited; then deemed that it might be better were we not to be found in the area, and so made off towards the College. As a matter of fact we need not have worried. We were the last people in anyone's mind. All we had done was, anonymously, to blow up the umpires.

'A' company and 'B' company had not even left their respective bases. The General and his staff were absolutely livid with anger and returned to their respective cars to travel back to London. Our Commanding Officer was in line for a rocket to end all rockets direct from the War Office. Parade was dismissed and many people had difficulty in keeping an appropriately straight face.

From now onwards the OTC virtually gave me up as a bad job – at best regarding me as a sort of 'albatross'. I was very much left to go my own way, provided that I saw that my behaviour was in no way flagrant. In any case, the things that were essential to my musical progress required more and more concentration. Eric Waddams had joined the staff; Bung had left to be replaced by a man called Norman Frayling. A boy called Michael Watts[5] – formerly head chorister at Llandaff Cathedral, with his treble voice still in superb maturity – was now in the Chapel choir, the repertoire was being changed beyond recognition, and I was expected to play for the full choral Evensong on Sundays once a month. Waddams himself sang on the bass line and a few other masters came forward to bolster the alto and tenor lines. Saturday Evensong now gave way to a full congregational rehearsal of the whole school which, little by little, began to perform its own parts of the services in better style . . . and the awful 'dragging' disappeared.

Frayling invited the Director of Music from Shrewsbury to come over and hear me play. I cannot now recall his name, but he was a man of dignity and authority while, nevertheless, having a very easy manner. He praised my playing and said that in his opinion I should prepare for a scholarship at the Royal Academy in London where, if lucky, I could benefit from the teaching of G.D. Cunningham who was to English organists what Marcel Dupré was to the French school. Furthermore, it would be good for me to get my own parish church appointment and learn the trade of choir training and dealing with the clergy the hard way. Needless to say, his remarks (and, obviously, a conversation with the Headmaster) carried the day, and my name was duly put forward to the Royal Academy for trial in the following Easter vacation. The Threlfall Scholarship could provide me with a full and free musical education for three years – provided I could manage to get it.

Scholarship examinations at the Royal Academy were to take place during the Easter vacation of 1939, and details of requirements for the Threlfall scholarship were duly forwarded. I would be required to play a work by Bach and a movement from one of the Sonatas of either Rheinberger or Mendelssohn. A theme would be submitted upon which I would be expected (if possible) to improvise; and there would be a viva voce discussion of my aspirations and the reasons for them. Preparation duly began and was taken really seriously by all involved. Frayling was both scrupulous and thorough, Waddams encouraging in every way. In the meantime a sad happening also proved in the end to be much to my benefit. Poor Hall was discovered somewhere in a state of total collapse and had to be brought back to the College and put to bed. A doctor was sent for and his sister appeared on the scene. A few days later he was taken away, never to reappear. Wiggins was left with the total management of the house on his hands until Frayling was appointed to be acting housemaster. That the Director of Music at Ellesmere should hold such a position was indeed a miracle, and one from which I was to find my life greatly facilitated. Easter came. I gained my scholarship and was given some carefully chosen advice by the Principal, Dr Stanley Marchant. I returned to a glorious summer term at Ellesmere, the more so because one now worked for the Oxford and Cambridge Exam in one's own time, or swam or lazed in the grounds as one wished. Suddenly Ellesmere College had become Blandings Castle – it was certainly in the right county! – and all was right with the world . . . except those wretched examinations at the end of term, but they seemed far enough away for the time being. Alas, I achieved distinction in music, honours in Latin and English, and failure in everything else.

The news came through while I was staying with my mother down on the Winchelsea Marsh. She said that the Headmaster had written to say that I could return for a further term in order to make up the subjects in which I had failed. This I refused to do. One of the subjects was mathematics in which I would have as much chance as the proverbial cat in hell. Then Hitler took his final one step too far and war was declared. I was due to be seventeen . . . anything could happen . . . I wanted as much of the Royal Academy as I could get.

Chapter V

War and the Grindstone

With the declaration of war the basic matters of life at once became an unpredictable problem. The Royal Academy, together with the College and all other public institutions in London, closed down. The same thing applied to all concert halls, art galleries, theatres and cinemas, and the plans for the mass evacuation of children were put into operation. Railways and all other forms of public transport were at once 'nationalised'. Hitler was blithely talking of a 'secret weapon', and Goering promised the immediate institution of air-raids at thirty minute intervals until the City of London and its environs were decimated. Any idea that the Romney Marsh was a safe haven was at once undermined by the information that, having broken through France, this was where the Germans would land in their invasion of England. All, of course, first-rate propaganda! Ideas of the solidity of the Maginot and Seigfried Lines began to dissolve rapidly.

In the end absolutely nothing happened. My mother, who stayed on after the Royal Academy and other places had sand-bagged themselves and reopened, heard a few heavy explosions from across the Channel; otherwise there was nothing to disturb this apparent peace. The 'phoney war' had begun. Theatres, concert halls, restaurants, all gradually reopened, hampered only by 'black-out' regulations and a tendency to keep to early hours. London Underground Stations, once the line was running beneath the earth's surface, became the most revolting 'night apartments' for those none too fastidious crowds who chose to use them. I took on voluntary watch duties at Southwark Cathedral, which consisted of prolonged visits to riverside pubs and going to bed in one of the vestries invariably well over the limit.

With the prospect of the Royal Academy being opened after all, I soon dropped my rather hypocritical 'duties' at Southwark. Having acquired a season ticket between Ealing Broadway and Paddington, with extension by Inner Circle to Baker Street, I began to haunt the Academy every day of the week. I was lucky. My organ professor was G.D.

Cunningham and I was placed with William Alwyn as a composition student. Alwyn, himself a flautist, had also composed some serious film scores which had earned him a wide reputation.

As to Cunningham, he was Birmingham City Organist, broadcast regularly for the BBC, and was a true virtuoso with the elastic conscience common to all virtuosi of that time, be they violinist, pianist, 'cellist, or what you will. He appeared annually at the Promenade Concerts and, jointly with Sir Henry Wood, contrived to produce the most spectacular and ear-splitting renditions of 'Handel Organ Concerti' known to God, man, or the old Queen's Hall. His playing of the formidable works of Liszt was utterly astounding. He played the organ works of Bach in the same way! Yet he was a wonderful teacher, the kindest and most sympathetic of men, and a staunch pacifist who made no attempt ever to escape the dangers of the bombs of London or Birmingham.

Tuesday afternoon was dedicated to the teaching and rehearsing of the Senior Orchestra, in which Henry Wood really showed his genius, demanding a truly high standard but always knowing when breaking point was reached and when to stop. His horn section was led by Dennis Brain with whom I formed a great friendship. The repertoire was usually one of single movements from a great variety of works, including opera excerpts and keyboard and string concerti, so that aspiring soloists might have their chance. I would sit enthralled in the half-deserted Hall, unless required to provide some (probably spurious) organ continuo. In those days, not only at the Royal Academy but also at public concerts in general, the harpsichord was a thing unknown, and all works written for that instrument were played on the piano.[6] I was in due course to have a blazing row with both Cunningham and Sir Henry on this very subject, which led to my undergoing a most unpleasant half-hour with the Warden. Of course, I was simply reduced to pulp and the threat of dismissal. (There were also fortnightly concerts in the Duke's Hall where senior students gave of their best – all good experience. For some reason, organ solos at these concerts were always placed at the beginning of the programme – as if to get them out of the way.)

The great thing for an organ student, from the point of view of practice facilities, was to get a church appointment. To use the organ in the Duke's Hall one had to pay a shilling an hour, and in any case the instrument was seldom available. It so happened that before Stanley Marchant had been appointed organist of St Paul's Cathedral, he had been at the ultra-fashionable church of St Peter's, Eaton Square. He knew the vicar and also that his organist successor was to be called up into the Air Force. So it was arranged that I should become Acting Organist with a choir of four semi-professional singers: alto, tenor, baritone and bass;

and so my practice problem was solved and I was, furthermore, earning a small stipend. This, combined with the occasional wedding fee of two guineas a time made me feel deceptively rich! The organ, like that at Southwark, was a fine instrument by Lewis. Alas, neither now exist, but there is still to be found one, smaller but similar, in the Church of St Barnabas in Tunbridge Wells.

So one continued to live in that fool's paradise of late adolescence, one's mind, like that of the man about to be hanged, most wonderfully concentrated. It was not until the débacle of May/June 1940 with the evacuation of Dunkirk and the capitulation of France that I and my fellow students really began to realise that the word 'war' meant precisely what it said. The land we held in Sussex was confiscated under compulsory purchase order, the whole of the Romney Marsh was declared to be a closed zone, mined and barb-wired throughout, and London began seriously to await its first attacks from the air.

Activities at the Royal Academy continued as usual and even the planned Promenade season at the Queen's Hall duly took place. There was the occasional air-raid, but these were very much damp squibs in comparison with what was to come. Guns banged furiously, the barrage balloons floated merrily, no German plane suffered, and it was all said to be very good for morale! I vaguely awaited my call-up papers and had been told by the Principal what to do on their receipt. The Royal Academy being an Institute of London University, I would almost certainly get a year's postponement in order to continue my studies. Eventually, in the autumn of that year, the papers arrived and that is exactly what happened. Finding myself unable to face the prospect of being at home during night raids, I joined the ARP as a messenger. This in no way interfered with my studies or my duties at St Peter's, but meant that I was up and out for two nights out of every three – apparently without ill effects, such is the stamina of youth. I was issued with a steel helmet and bicycle, and expected to carry out such duties as were requested by the Warden. At this stage we were too far away from London itself for this to be of any worry.

Meanwhile Cunningham kept my nose firmly to the grindstone, seeing to it that I played pieces at as many of the Academy concerts as possible. I found that I had a particularly retentive memory and made it a point of honour with myself never to play recitals other than in this manner. After all, as Dupré was to say to me some years later, 'any fool can do his sight-reading in public.' I recall, on consecutive days, (though how this came about I cannot now remember) playing a Bach Trio Sonata[7] and the great E flat Fugue that closes the *Clavierübung*. I was in due course sent for by the Principal and congratulated.

At St Peter's, I arduously disciplined my style of service accompaniment, going frequently to weekday Evensong at the Abbey, sitting in the organ loft with Bullock, and observing everything minutely. The services were sung by the lay-vicars only, the choristers having been evacuated to Christ's Hospital, near Horsham. (Those of St Paul's Cathedral were now resident and singing at Truro). Then two things happened: the Abbey Dean and Chapter closed the choir school, and Bullock – his house already blown to bits – resigned in justifiable fury. Who can possibly blame him? But he had meanwhile discovered that in addition to my acting-appointment at Eaton Square, I had become assistant to Ralph Downes at Brompton Oratory. Scathingly, he dismissed me: 'Like the Vicar of Bray! If you can't get to heaven one way, you'll get there the other.' I never saw him again.

When I discovered the Oratory, it must have been a red-letter Saint's Day. I could not understand what was going on, not because it was in Latin, but because the liturgy was foreign to me. (I had yet to come across the Anglo-Catholics – more Catholic than the Pope!) The organ voluntary at the conclusion was one of the Bach/Vivaldi concertos, played in a manner of such poise, authority and commitment, that I was utterly astounded. I went to the door under the gallery and waited for Ralph Downes to appear. When he did, I asked him if I might see the organ console and told him diffidently who I was. There was none of the 'great man' about him that I had come to associate with Anglican cathedral organists. He took me upstairs, asked me all about myself and my ambitions, discovered that we both lived in Ealing, that we both came from Derbyshire families, that we were both fascinated by steam railway traction. We travelled homeward together on the District Line from South Kensington and he said that he would like to hear me play. Perhaps I could meet him one evening at the Oratory when the church was closed. He explained how he was attempting to revoice the large Bishop organ more on the lines of Cavaillé-Coll. It might be that I could help him, for which I would of course be paid; and in due course I was appointed his salaried sub-organist. Although he was eighteen years my senior, he became and remained a mentor and one of my closest friends until his death in 1993.

I now began to find that despite my convictions that I would one day be a cathedral organist, there were tremendous holes in the knowledge required if I were to be anything more than the limited and somewhat feeble compromise that could then be encountered in almost any such post. Liturgical matters apart, the first of the musical limitations to face me was the matter of plainsong. It is true that in cathedrals and a number of parish churches one might hear the men's voices (even boys' voices in the extreme Anglo-Catholicism of places like All Saints, Margaret Street) chanting the psalms to the psalter as set out by Briggs and Frere.

But the eight tones had all been brutally corrupted with banishment of flexes, abrupt – i.e. broken – mediations, and arbitrary use of endings that took no account of the final (that is to say, the UT) of the mode concerned. Chanting would be casually 'speech rhythm' rather than syllabic, and in more elaborate chant, that of antiphons or texts of the Communion Service, melismata would be forced on to syllables that were inevitably of the wrong formation and thus productive of the most grotesque results. Combined with this was the matter of correct organ accompaniment, and since every aspect of the music had its foundation in the text (Latin, of course) the Church of England was not only in a cleft stick, but likely to remain so while people continued to pretend that the problems did not exist. This was just not going to be good enough for any cathedral where I might have charge of the music. Thus the Oratory, from the point of view of musical and liturgical scholarship, was providing me with an aspect of my education not to be found in those formally recognised colleges and academies geared to the tuition of purely secular musicians. As to my eternal soul, in no way did those 'wicked Romans' ever try to question or persuade me in any way whatsoever, friendly though they might be.

In addition to gaining a gradually increasing knowledge of melismatic chant, I also came to understand its notation – something which on first appearance would seem to be utterly indecipherable with its strange squirls, its four line stave, its two moveable clefs – but which, in fact, was the essence of simplicity. And then there was the great polyphonic school of the Renaissance which had gradually derived from it. At that time HMV still marketed Palestrina's *Missa Assumpta est Maria* sung by the Mâitrise de Dijon under the direction of Monseigneur Samson, and also various other examples recorded by the Sistine Choir directed by the redoubtable Lorenzo Perosi. The Dijon choir was one of absolutely integrated voices such as we were not to hear in this country until the advent of George Malcolm at Westminster Cathedral; Perosi's Sistine choir on the other hand was remarkable for a fine careless rapture, a searing passion, and a nice disregard for any such things as intonation and ensemble. Clearly the Holy Ghost would look after all that! I bought all these records and played them daily, eventually managing to acquire scores of most of the works through J.W. Chester of Malborough Street. Of English cathedral music, nothing was available except the special and very unsatisfactory recordings of the complete 1937 Coronation Service. But from that service came one particular thing: Vaughan Williams' magnificent F major setting of the *Te Deum* which, in due course, I was to introduce into the repertoire at Ely, to be sung at Matins on such major Feasts as Christmas Day, Easter, and Whitsunday.

Gradually my life became choked with activity and I absorbed knowledge and grasped experience with a sort of desperation that is only possible to a youth working under that ever unspoken stress – for every day that I awoke might, for all I knew, prove to be my last. So, to be attached to the ARP post for two nights and to alternate these with a post-Benediction to late evening session, endeavouring to help Ralph Downes on his work at the Oratory organ, having spent the day itself in practising or attendance at the Academy, I continued to live life as it were to the full. The air raids had gradually become a pattern, though one that was very mild when compared with what was to come. My bad time was each third night because for some reason I could never bear to be in a house when there was a raid in progress. To be in church, in the Duke's Hall, or patrolling the streets was alright. But those third nights, even though I had a bed made up under the grand piano, were no better than episodes of sheer terror. As to listening to concerts after dark, this was out of the question. The BBC with its Symphony Orchestra had been evacuated to Bedford and, of course, their concerts were broadcast in the evening. Meanwhile Goering's jolly fellows would have started their night's work on the London docks. Then came the appalling night when they decided to destroy the City. I am still able through memory's eye to see, eastward and miles from myself, that dirty and ruddy glow that made nonsense of the darkness of a night sky. Hitler was in no hurry and was simply working step by step as required by his inexorable plan.

As the Blitz attacks moved gradually towards the West End of London, I became uncomfortably aware of a fact that was eventually going to affect myself in the ARP and also, through the sheer inaccuracy of the German bombers, the town of Ealing. Between Paddington and Ealing Broadway, over a vast area, lay the Great Western Railway's freight marshalling yard, the fourth biggest marshalling yard in the country. Anything to do with transport was, naturally, fair game, but if this marshalling yard could be crippled then unimaginable problems of distribution would be the result and the whole of the West London Joint Railway would become virtually useless. Of course, this part of the scheme was duly put into action and, except for the occasional night off so that Liverpool, Manchester, Birmingham and, most notably, Coventry could be bombed, our friends the Huns never failed to pay us a visit. They never hit the yard or its appurtenances once, but they did hit just about everything else around it. Every evening at dusk the sirens would wail; there would be no respite until dawn of the next day.

My duties as an ARP messenger meant precisely what the words said. Thus it came about that I was required to take some document or papers to a neighbouring post somewhere in the direction of Ealing Common.

The sirens had given their alarm sometime previously and we were already under Red Alert. I donned my steel helmet, collected my gas mask and bicycle, and duly set off. Not much relishing my task, I began to pedal strenuously, gathering speed. Then I heard the bomb coming down.

Now we had all been given careful instruction as to what to do in such circumstances. If the sound of the bomb's descent was steady, then it would probably be going to land outside the area of immediate danger – though it would be as well not to take any chances. But if the sound was ever increasing, the drill was to throw oneself downwards on the ground with one's face against the back of one's hands and to commend oneself to God or one's Guardian Angel or whatever.

Well that awful whistling was increasing, and that rapidly. I flung myself from the bike and onto the ground in the prescribed manner, twisting the handlebars, barking my knees and shins, grazing my knuckles, and waited. To my surprise, there was absolute silence. Cautiously and painfully I gathered myself together, got up and straightened the handlebars, and stood still. Perhaps the explosion of the bomb had coincided with my fall from the bike. But there was no sound of any plane, nor were any guns firing. Dazed, I remounted my bicycle and, badly shaken, recommenced my journey.

I thought, 'I don't like this – let's get it over,' and increased my speed accordingly. Then, damnation, the same thing happened all over again. There it was – the unmistakable and ever increasing whistle, gathering, piercing, intensifying. What in hell were the Germans playing at? Again I hit the ground – probably harder than before. Again, as I came to, I became aware of nothing but absolute silence. Then, sitting on the road, the solution occurred to me. The steel helmets contained an inner close-fitting headpiece, buffered from the helmet itself by pads of rubber insulation. The faster I chose to cycle, the more keenly the draught whistled its way through the aperture thus available.

I remounted, slowly delivered my message or whatever it was and, as slowly, cycled back to my own base. As I entered, one of the Wardens said: 'We seem to be having a remarkably quiet night tonight.' I was given a mug of tea freely laced with tinned Carnation milk.

Then one morning I went to St Peter's, Eaton Square, intending to do some organ practice before going on to the Academy. There was a certain odour in the air which seemed unpleasantly familiar, and turning a corner I came upon the church, left not bombed but blasted. Not a window left, the ceiling riddled, the arcaded porch pock marked and, lying on a dust sheet inside the main entrance, the body of the vicar – apparently unharmed, just asleep never to awaken again. I remember the moment. I am still surprised that I felt nothing – not even a sort of vacuum. I telephoned Dr Stanley Marchant, knowing of their long acquaintance. A few days later we both, with many others, attended the funeral amidst all the dirt and rubble which could not, in any way, detract from the timeless dignity of the Prayer Book language.

I now suffered a severe drop in income for, as acting-organist, St Peter's was under no obligation to me. But there were many churches losing their organists to the Forces, and constant enquiries coming to the Academy. One such was from a Father Evans of St Mark's, Marylebone Road, and I went to see him. There was also a Church Warden present – the people's Warden – and they both lost no time in putting me at my ease. I was grateful to be given the appointment (at the usual sort of stipend), the church was a pleasing and dignified building, and the organ a small but beautifully voiced instrument by Whitely. Practice time was available to me as and when I wanted it, the principal service on Sundays was a fully robed Sung Eucharist with incense and candles, the singing a simple plainsong as there was no choir. The hymns were of the best chosen from the English Hymnal.

By now I knew that I had a clear year to run, my call-up having been officially postponed on the lines suggested to me by Stanley Marchant. I also found that the People's Warden was very much musically inclined, so I outlined to him a plan whereby the music of the Eucharist could be considerably enhanced. It would be quite possible for me to collect a regular students' choir of two sopranos with alto, tenor and bass, provided that they could be paid some sort of expense fees. Holland (I now recall his name) was all for this and we took the matter to Father Evans. He too was in agreement – so it was a matter of getting it past the church council, which fortunately was done without difficulty.

I well remember that choir, my very first, though the only name I recall is that of the bass John Lanchberry – as crazy about the music of Stravinsky as I was myself, and a musician who was to go on to make a great name for himself conducting both in the Opera House and with the Royal Ballet. As to repertoire, we built on Palestrina, Byrd, Viadana and occasionally Mozart. Of course, all texts had to be the correct English ones, causing me great headaches in wresting music from its original Latin with as little damage as possible. We were, however, permitted to sing motets in Latin as they ranked as extra-liturgical.

St Mark's gradually gained something of a reputation for itself for, naturally, any sort of music in war-time London parish churches was at a low ebb. But in due course my call-up papers arrived and I was required to present myself at a depot in Hounslow for medical examination. A kindly doctor asked me about myself and what I had been doing, and then proceeded to get on with the routine business of a full physical check. After a while he came back to listening to my chest, taking infinite pains, and then sent away for another doctor who proceeded to do the same thing. They then both retired in consultation. A third doctor came and listened all round my chest and then he too joined them. My original doctor asked me if I had ever had rheumatic fever, and upon receiving a negative answer they proceeded to consult some more. I was beginning to feel somewhat worried and must certainly have shown it when the first doctor came back to me and said 'I am afraid we shall have to excuse you from military service. There is a leaking valve in your heart.' He hastened to put my mind at rest, saying that many people had this deficiency, that as a musician of highly strung temperament it was better that I should continue with my professional training, and that I would therefore be registered as being Grade IV. Meanwhile in avoiding excess of physical strain there was no reason why I should not live as long as anyone else. So it was back to St Mark's, back to the Academy with another full year of scholarship to run, back to assisting Ralph Downes, and back to the ARP which was becoming less and less of a casual pastime; but overall a basic relief in knowing that I could get on without interruption in the direction I had set for myself. However, sadness and troubles were looming: one by one my close student friends disappeared into the Forces and Father Evans died.

There was the usual clerical interregnum at St Mark's while we all wondered how things would work out under the new man. In fact, they could not have been worse. He was a High Churchman who sweated profusely in his anxiety to please, was all for glorious music as far as I was concerned, deplored it as far as those in the congregation who chose to grumble were concerned, was a miracle of non-commitment when Holland told him he was making a rod for his own back, and all in all left one with about as much feeling of security as a jellied eel. In the end opportunity played into his hands and he wasted no time in taking advantage of it.

During the war, as had been the case in any other war, sexual morals tended to reach an ebb. Decent girls kept themselves to themselves. We male youngsters wanted to know – not to form a relationship, simply 'to know'. After all, any one of us might be called up and shot or, failing that, not even get through the coming night if the air-raiding happened to come too close in our direction. And there were plenty of girls around who did not fancy the idea of call-up and peeling potatoes, and could avoid this should they get married. One such split on me. She went to St Mark's and told the vicar. His reaction was all that she could have desired. She was not pregnant. It was the 'fact' that mattered. So he telephoned her father and he telephoned my mother. He let it be known that the only way for the matter to be put in order was for us to be married, otherwise he would be in duty bound to inform the Principal of the Academy and I would lose my scholarship. Meanwhile, I must cease to play for services and the choir would be dismissed. Through ignorance of my own rights, he had won hands down!

Without delay, the vicar conducted a 'marriage service'. For me that was the end of it all and I never saw the interior of that beautiful little church again. It was 1943 and I was faced with two intense problems: where could I find an instrument for regular practising and how could I stand living under the same roof with someone whose every remark and every domestic incompetence made me cringe. Also I was filled with a reluctance to face other people: it never occurring to me that anyone else could possibly have got themselves 'landed' as I seemed to have done. Seeking some professional relief as a musician, I went to see a curate I knew at the Church of St Alban in Holborn. He had formerly been Precentor of Tewkesbury Abbey, and I therefore felt there would be a real chance of some common ground. The terrible words of Bernard Shaw: 'Middle class morality claims another victim' sounded in my ears and I was in no way going to settle for that. I made an appointment with Father Taylor at St Alban's and duly went and told him as much of my story as I felt he ought to know.

Chapter VI

Tewkesbury Abbey

So, this smart new Vicar at St Mark's had dismissed the choir. Naturally, that made it quite impossible that I should stay on as his organist. I must be found another berth without delay. Father Taylor mused awhile. He knew that Father Brian, the Vicar of Tewkesbury, would be seeking another organist in the near future. Did I know Tewkesbury Abbey? Would I have any objection to leaving London? He could certainly write to Father Brian about me. Should I go to Tewkesbury, I would at least be working for a gentleman! And, as a building, it was one of the most marvellous churches in England, surpassing even some of those that were of cathedral rank.

His words took my mind back to the previous Easter Monday when I had fulfilled my long established vow to visit Ely. I had spent most of the day exploring the cathedral and its miraculous Lady Chapel – only about half the length of, but five feet wider than the chapel of King's College, Cambridge. The canticles at Evensong had been sung both thinly and indifferently to Wood in E flat (not one of his happiest efforts), the anthem I could not remember, and the organ voluntary had been the first movement from the *Symphonie Romane* by Widor – a work based strictly on the plainchant of the Easter antiphon *Haec dies quam fecit Dominus*. Marmaduke Conway, the then organist, had shown remarkable virtuosity in his playing of this piece. I awaited him afterwards at the foot of the organ loft stairs and asked if I might be allowed to see the console. Dr Conway was surprisingly casual ... 'Yes, go upstairs if you want to,' and he just walked away.

I kept all Tewkesbury Abbey thoughts to myself, confiding only in Ralph Downes. Behaving in a sort of planned contradiction, I gazed hungrily at the photographs that appeared in Crossley's book on English Abbeys while, simultaneously, pretending to banish the whole subject from my mind. Idly, I kept an eye on the *Church Times* for such appointments as might be advertised in that paper – almost dreading that there might be something for which I *ought* to apply while, myself, having no enthusiasm for the post. Then, one day, a letter arrived bearing the Tewkesbury post mark. This would have been during early July in 1943. The Vicar of Tewkesbury wrote saying that he would be making a new appointment to the post of organist at the Abbey, duties to commence during the autumn of that year, that he had been having some correspondence with Father Taylor of St Alban's, Holborn, and that he understood that I might be interested in discussing the matter with him. If so, would I please travel down from Paddington to Cheltenham on the date he suggested and he would meet me there and drive me to Tewkesbury. I should come prepared to stay overnight. I replied to his letter at once, cancelled any engagements I may have had over the relevant days, gritted my teeth for silence, and somehow managed to get through the necessary time of waiting without exploding.

The train was, of course, the *Cheltenham Flyer* of pre-war fame, though in rather dirtier condition than the Great Western itself would ever have countenanced. But fly it did, and in due course I alighted from the traditional remains of the four coaches hauled by a Prairie Tank. A pleasant and welcoming middle-aged clergyman was waiting at the barrier to meet me. As we set off on the road from Cheltenham I began to get my first impressions of Cotswold countryside, while he told me of the town to which we were going, of its famous bridge where the Severn and the Avon meet, of the house where he lived and where I would be staying – formerly the Abbot's House and approached through a great stone gateway. We arrived, but on getting out of the car, he at once took me to the Abbey West Door. Throwing open a small portal, he simply said: 'Look' – and I breathtakingly saw before me the whole length of the church, through its Norman and crouch-vaulted nave and across to its decorated vaulted choir. We then went into lunch. To my amazement, late wartime though it was, we were waited upon by three most presentable young girls, each wearing a pale green frock with white apron and head-cap. Clearly, the Vicar of Tewkesbury was a person who believed in doing things well.

After luncheon I was escorted to my room. Whereas the ancient frontage of the Abbey House, with its famous oriel window, faces North, the house itself in fact faces South and this together with its independent frontage is Georgian, dating from the 1790s. The room I had been given was central, facing a great ash tree. My luggage had been unpacked and, by the sonorous sounds of the bells striking from the Abbey tower, I knew that it was half-past two. I made my way downstairs for the first part of my interview with Father Brian.

If the room in which he greeted me was intended as a vast sitting room and study, there was extending East from it yet another comfortable room with tasteful prints and pictures on the walls and an enticing looking grand piano; I suppose it was what was properly called a 'withdrawing' room. We sat down on either side of the fireplace, the afternoon was warm, and I was exceedingly nervous. I asked permission to smoke a cigarette and was handed a carved box and a lighter. But shortly after a few puffs I felt my concentration was ebbing, and I threw my stub end into what appeared to be a neatly tidied fireplace. To my horror, within a matter of seconds, we were both sitting in front of a cheerfully blazing fire, such was the efficiency of the green-frocked young ladies! Father Brian just took one look at me and proceeded to roar with laughter. I suppose it is tautology to say that the incident 'broke the ice'.

We did not bother to go into my past history as a musician; clearly all this had already been thoroughly checked. What was of first importance was that I should be put into the unvarnished picture vis-à-vis Tewkesbury itself. The services on a Sunday were Litany in procession followed by a Solemn Eucharist, and Evensong in the late afternoon. The Eucharist was sung to Merbecke, Anglican chants were used for Evensong. Hymns were from the English Hymnal and were chosen by the Vicar himself. There were practice sessions for the boys after school on three days each week. The men, consisting of *no* alto, two tenors and three basses, had not attended a choir practice since the beginning of the war, and refused to go out in the black-out. As I knew, there were two organs in the Abbey and both were available to me for my own purposes at any time I wished up to ten o'clock at night, excepting when services might be being said. Lights from either organ console did not interfere with the blackout regulations, but I would need a torch to get around the building, and I would have to see that all electricity mains were turned off at the end of any session of work. Did I know about the two organs? We would be going over to the church shortly, so that I could make their acquaintance. There would also be a boys' rehearsal so that I could meet the choristers who numbered some sixteen altogether.

At this stage, I knew all about the two organs, and it is a bitter irony that I in fact should be the last organist of Tewkesbury to know them in practice for what they truly were. That standing on the south side of the choir was a double organ (two choruses playable from separate keyboards) by Renatus Harris. It had been built for Magdelen College, Oxford, and later moved to Tewkesbury. A pedal board with 16ft bourdon and couplers had been added in the nineteenth century by Willis, thus making it an ideal instrument in every way for the music of Bach, as well as for English music of the appropriate times. The organ in the north transept was by Michell and Thynne, built for and displayed at the Inventions Exhibition in 1885. Its specification, over pedal and four keyboards, is a triumph of economy, its voicing convincing in nine-teenth-century romantic music either French or German, its action making it a pleasure upon which to play. Alas, it failed to appeal at the time and ruined its builders. Eventually it was bought and presented to the Abbey by the Reverend C.W. Grove of Mythe House, Tewkesbury, in commemoration of the Jubilee of Queen Victoria in 1887. Shortly after my time at Tewkesbury a 'grand scheme' was put in train, whereby the Harris organ was extended and revoiced beyond recognition, its action removed and replaced with an electric system whereby it could be played from a modern detached console on the north side of the choir, in conjunction with new and amorphous pipe choruses speaking from diverse parts of the building. The Michell and Thynne organ, being considered superfluous to requirements, was left to stand in silence and rot. Let me at once add that the firm of organ builders involved in all this were in no way to be held to blame. They were called in to obey the orders of a single private individual, and cannot themselves be held responsible.

However, this is to anticipate. Father Brian offered me the post at a salary of £150 per annum and said that arrangements would be made for the accommodation of myself and my wife. I would be expected to begin my duties at the beginning of October. Of course I was thrilled, accepted, and returned to London on the next day in the agreement that I was now organist designate. Upon arrival at Paddington, I took a taxi straight to the Royal Academy and told the Principal, noting that it meant my resigning my scholarship. He was wonderfully delighted, talked to me about not trying to do too much in a hurry, and sent me away with his best wishes.

It is of vital importance that I never forget precisely what I owe to my all too short time at Tewkesbury. I was able to, and did, practise daily upon the superb instruments; I came to find that although I got on well with small boys I knew nothing about the training of treble voices; I was soaked in superb architecture and glorious countryside; I desperately missed the polyphony that we used to sing at my church in London; I found a great and kindly friend in Herbert Sumsion who was organist of Gloucester Cathedral and whose organ loft I used to visit twice a week, often being invited to play the concluding voluntary; the three smartly clad servant girls, suddenly being called up to war-work, I found a self-contained home in their former quarters in the Abbey House.

But life was by no means simple. Not one of my choristers had any sight-reading ability nor would any of them consider learning the piano. The choirmen simply gave me a wide berth. By rote, I managed to teach the boys Wesley's Evening Canticles in F and, when eventually they came to sing them one Sunday evening, I tactfully placed copies in the men's stalls although fully aware that the printed pages would to them be quite meaningless. The boys did their best but their simple best was desecrated at various points by the men deliberately braying such notes as might come into their heads. It drove me to the verge of tears, but the storm came afterwards.

One of the men – obviously a token spokesman – waylaid me and asked me what did I, a mere boy, think that I was doing? 'We,' he continued, 'we have known this place all our lives and we have it in our hearts.' Simultaneously, members of the congregation bombarded Father Brian but of this he made no mention to me. But he did show me a letter from one of the parents strongly complaining that Mr Howard seemed to think that he had a prior call upon the boys in any way that might suit himself.

A Mrs Wyatt and her husband were intrigued by my enthusiasms for the music of Byrd and Palestrina. They invited me to meet them in their home twice each week so that I might teach and coach them and two of their friends in Palestrina's *Missa Brevis*. The Wyatts sang alto and bass, the soprano was adequate, the tenor excellent and, furthermore, he could sight-read. Eventually I suggested how exciting it would be to hear this music in the reverberant acoustic of the Abbey – but sadly this was not possible. The tenor was a non-conformist, he had never set foot inside the Abbey church, and he would never do so.

Meanwhile the domestic front became daily more and more a torture and an acute embarrassment. My 'partner' was given to sudden and frequent bursts of hysterical rowing which must have been audible all over the Abbey House. Then began the habitual visits to the tap room of the Bell Hotel from which she would return in a state of drooling bonhomie, frequently bringing with her a pathetic wreck of an old man who claimed to be (and probably was) an Old Etonian. He was also much given to 'seeing things' and weeping. Then came the evening when she turned up with a stalwart American GI who insisted on addressing me as 'Sir'. This brought about rapid and unexpected reactions.

A lady from the congregation called, asking if she could see me privately on a matter of some delicacy. She suggested that I might be wise not to admit a 'certain American' to my home. He was not a desirable character and was already known to be having an affair with a local married woman whose husband was away serving with the Forces. I said that I took her meaning and thanked her.

But when I came to mention the business to 'Mrs Howard', the fat was well and truly in the fire. In a rage that virtually cracked my ear drums, she slammed out of the house and showed no sign of returning.

After a while I dragged myself over to the Abbey and sought distraction and consolation in hard work. I also changed all the bedding (much overdue) and generally set out to make the place more tidy. I was fraught with humiliation, but no one remarked on her absence although everyone must have known. Then, after some four or five days, she reappeared all smiles as if I ought to be overjoyed to see her.

She had been to London – not to her parents – but to my mother who had doubtless been only too pleased to see the back of her. As far as I was concerned, I was merely sorry to have what had been for me such a fruitful interlude brought to an end. But together with my Bach repertoire I was well into the mastery of Vierne's Second Symphony and had begun exploratory work into the technical demands of his Fifth. Later, Father Brian was to tell someone that the perpetual sounds of the Abbey organs nearly drove him insane!

Clearly, from a choral point of view, Tewkesbury was for me a total non-starter. What *was* there for me was the cultural fascination of the building itself and the opportunity (perhaps never to come again) to develop a first class organ technique and to build a comprehensive and virtuoso repertoire. To some extent my choral thirst could be satisfied by my constant visits to the organ-loft of Gloucester Cathedral and the kindly friendship of Herbert Sumsion. But there was little Tudor or Jacobean music sung there and the lists tended to be full of people like Blaire, Brewer, Atkins, and other (to me, utterly fatuous) hangovers from the recent past.

Sumsion, on more than one occasion, travelled over from Gloucester to Tewkesbury to see me, obviously deriving that pleasure enjoyed by professional musicians when they are able to talk 'shop' together. We would saunter around the Abbey and its surrounding grounds, deeply engrossed in the things that truly mattered to us – he always treating me with the great kindness of a senior towards an enthusiastic junior. To my wife's pert and over familiar behaviour he always adopted that well mannered poise which seems to be unaware of such unfortunate conduct. But for my part, I was all too often suffused with painfully acute embarrassment. Yet Sumsion's kindliness to me never wavered. He was, indeed, an absolute bastion in circumstances so fraught and humiliating.

All of this made me think, and the more I did, so did I come to realise the incredible ignorance and neglect of the great Renaissance and Reformation schools of music in our churches and cathedrals. The whole idea of what was to become The Renaissance Society began to take shape in my mind, and I set up urgent contact with those in London whom I knew would help and support me. I was driven by an inner compulsion so strong that when Herbert Sumsion told me of changes due at Gloucester, and invited me to become his assistant organist at the Cathedral, I had to refuse and also to take him into my confidence. He was in no way convinced that I was doing the right thing. In due course, I had to resign from the Abbey to the grave displeasure of Father Brian, and duly returned to London and the bombs.

Interlude: Nights of Gestation

I arrived in London utterly exhausted yet, such was my sense of antic-ipation, quivering like an aspen leaf. Since the previous Christmas and up to my departure in April from Gloucestershire I had been resorting to my former student/ARP/Oratory habits – but this time it had been organ practice during the day and brain-racking clerical work at night; bed at dawn and arising mid-morning; my only alleviation, trips to Gloucester Cathedral and the thrill one day of hearing there the wonder-ful tonal astringency of Tallis' 'dorian' *Magnificat and Nunc Dimittis*.

The fact that I heard the Tallis Canticles at all shows that the day must have been a Friday. At that time it was customary for cathedrals to treat Fridays as a day of semi-penitence and so Evensong would be sung unaccompanied, not even a preamble or postlude being played on the organ. Thus the use of Tudor and Jacobean music was virtually enforced. (Its other purpose appeared to be sporadic use during Lent and particularly Holy Week.) Otherwise it was the by now conventional diet – rancid Victorian and Edwardian musical pomp and the faceless contemporary. Thus were Taverner, Tallis, Byrd, Weelkes, Morley and their contemporaries down-graded. But, as I had discovered through my great good fortune in being assistant to Downes, such was not the case in responsible foundations in the Roman Catholic Church.

In 1903 Pope Pius X had issued a *Motu Proprio* ordering a 'spring cleaning' of the music used in the Catholic Church. The fashionable but ultra-sickly and sanctimonious motets and mass settings must go, and were to be replaced by works matching that sheer finesse and liturgical integrity innate in Italian and Tudor polyphony. And in the mid-1930s, with the appointment of Henry Washington as Choirmaster and Director of Music at Brompton Oratory, this was precisely the programme that was so scrupulously put into operation.

Put like this, the attitude of the Anglican church began to appear somewhat pathetic. After all, one could scarcely regard Palestrina's radiant *Missa Assumpta est Maria* as a penitential work! Likewise Byrd's 'Sing joyfully unto God our strength' and Gibbons' 'O clap your hands', with its thrilling deployment of double choir work, are hardly breast-beating material. As far as the Church of England was concerned, it seemed that it was only Boris Ord of King's, Cambridge, who was not blinkered by this sad but so turn-of-the-century English sack-cloth-and-ashes attitude. As to scholarship, one heard organ accompaniments played where they should not have been played, and omitted where they should have been forming an integral part of the music. With Restoration and pre-Restoration music there was no sense of re-creation: no sense that the words informed the music and that the singers should be a vehicle whereby new life was breathed into the music with every individual performance. Just four beats to the bar and, if you were lucky, a bit of a *rallentando* at the end.

I worked all these thoughts and conclusions into a sort of manifesto and sent a copy to almost every Dean, Provost and Cathedral Organist in the country, with the further information that I proposed to take steps at whatever cost to myself to expose the situation by public demonstration. The acknowledgements were few, some of them ill-mannered. Stanley Marchant sent me a brief note saying that he could see no need for 'an organ music society of this nature'. He was obviously displeased that I should not be pursuing my career along acceptably conventional lines. I never found out what he meant by 'organ music society'. It was also pointed out to me that the music for which I was showing so much concern was intended for liturgical use and not for performance in secular concerts where the prime object could only be 'entertainment of the public'.

Of course this latter point played straight into my hands for, as far as the Church of England was concerned, there could be no question of 'entertainment of the public'. The public did not even know that such music existed, let alone of the message that it might carry to them. The Dean of Guildford said in a recent sermon: 'There is little that human beings can make that is more powerful than music to draw men to God, to unite them in his Service and to lift them into His Presence.' To which I would add the reminder that the words are in the music and the music is in the words. In failing to respect this, the remnant can only be 'a sounding brass or a tinkling cymbal'. As the chaplain at Ellesmere had pointedly said to me: 'The best is good enough for God.'

So I continued my nocturnal vigils, now turning to other aspects of the problem. I knew that I was assured of a nucleus of practical support from a rather limited number of singers in London, some of whom were past acquaintances and others who had already worked with me when I had been organist of St Mark's Church, Marylebone Road. But these people were not sufficient in themselves for the makings of a chamber choir to sing a comprehensive repertoire. Furthermore, there was the inescapable fact that I would be trying to communicate my message by means of an instrument already at fault with itself: for the top line would be one of sopranos, not boy choristers, and the alto line would be composed of contraltos, not counter-tenors. There was nothing that I could do about this except hope that the public (if any) would not look a gift horse in the mouth. I had by now so far committed myself that there could be no turning back, and I asked all my London colleagues to look out diligently for singers – especially tenors and basses – who would be prepared to meet me both for audition and discussion. My great, as it were, missionary point would be that nothing like this had ever been done before. Fine choirs there were, yes: the Glasgow Orpheus, the Fleet Street Singers, the BBC Singers – but these were in no way specialist groups. My choir was to be one of strictly set purpose and no deviation would be permitted. The enterprise was not merely one of desperation, it was also unique.

Gradually, in this end-of-the-war and music starved London, I met many possible singers – amateurs of a competence and quality which it would be hard to find today. Among my selection were city business-men, bankers, medical students, accountants and women recently from either the RCM, the RAM, or Trinity College: secretaries, school mistresses, nurses. One young soprano was still studying at the Royal Academy and would, therefore, have to get formal permission. I went with her to see her professor and he in turn went to see the Principal. He returned looking simply amazed. 'I asked Sir Stanley,' he said, 'saying that I had no objection, and he replied: "No. Certainly not with those people." Whatever can he have meant?'

The really awkward line was the alto, for in no way does the contralto voice correspond in range and timbre to the counter-tenor. Try what I might, this line was never truly acceptable during the comparatively short time in which I maintained it. Sopranos were an easier matter and an authentic solution was eventually found to that problem many years later. It is sufficient here to say that by the Spring of 1944 we were poised and ready to go. As to what the future held, I had no idea. With typical Howard impetuosity, I had burned my boats.

Chapter VII

The Renaissance Singers and Christ Church, Woburn Square

So came about the formation of the Renaissance Society, with its performing arm, The Renaissance Singers. It numbered among its vice-presidents The Very Reverend A.S. Duncan-Jones, Dean of Chichester, and The Right Reverend Colin Dunlop, Bishop of Jarrow, later to become Dean of Lincoln. The eventual president was Vaughan Williams. Bound by strict constitution the chairman was Roy Bridge, a senior official of the Bank of England, and I (with wide ranging powers) was Director of the whole organisation. The purpose of the Society was 'by advocacy and example' to promote a proper liturgical revival of the music of the great masters of the Renaissance, the Reformation, and the Restoration Schools. H.A. Hawkins of Chichester was the only cathedral organist to take the venture seriously, writing a most kindly note of encouragement to me and expressing a hope that I might be able to visit him in the not too distant future.

Meanwhile I had rented an upper maisonette in a pleasing but somewhat decayed terrace in Philbeach Gardens near Earls Court Station. It was very much a case of 'Queen Anne front and Mary Anne back' for behind ran a limb of the West London Joint Railway. This meant that at any hour, but particularly during the night, one could be disturbed by cattle trains grinding to a halt, the clanging of buffers, the mooing of cows and the pathetic bleating of sheep – animals making their last journey on earth and one knew only too well to where they were going.

I chose to make the main front room my bedroom, work room and library. The top floor I sublet to a 'cellist and his wife, thus slightly easing my financial burdens. My wife continued her practice of disappearing from time to time. Where she went I do not know, but it was certainly not to my mother in Ealing. Then one day having cause to go into the rear room I found that the bed was crawling with lice. The Sanitory Inspector responded promptly to my telephone call and the whole bed was taken away to be burned. My 'partner' duly returned and seemed to be perfectly happy with a mattress on the floor. But mercifully I had other and greater things to occupy my mind.

Officially the birth of the Renaissance Society dated from March 1944, and I already had a nucleus of singers around which to start building a fully voiced choir. The alto line, at this stage, consisted entirely of contraltos. As I recall, the first public recital to be given by the Renaissance Singers took place, after much arduous rehearsal, in the July of that year. The location was a somewhat bomb-scarred Marylebone Parish Church opposite the Royal Academy of Music, and the principal work in the programme was Palestrina's *Missa Brevis*. London was comparatively speaking music starved at that time, and this enormous church was absolutely packed. A retiring 'silver' collection produced for the Society its first funds. The event was ignored by the Press.

It seems strange now to recall that this recital had been dependent almost entirely upon street advertising. Felix Aprahamian, a friend and Musical Consultant, had advised me about this, and the printing and distribution of double-crown posters was undertaken by Vail and Co, so that in central London it was virtually impossible to pass a fenced-off bombed site without coming across the words 'Music of the Polyphonic Era – The Renaissance Singers'. Newspaper advertising was costly, and anyway, *which* newspapers, *The Times* apart? But I think that even to Our Music Critic, as well as those of other papers, the Polyphonic Era was probably thought of as being something to do with those soul-destroying exercises one was expected to work for the degree of B. Mus. Not really a living thing at all!

It was also due to the enthusiasm and active work of Felix Aprahamian that we came to the notice of the French Cultural Attaché, and this led to our participation in a *Concert Spirituel* arranged by him. We began the programme with a Mass by Lassus entitled *Puisque jay perdu*. After the *Kyries*, the *Gloria* was intoned, and the choir took up the music with the words *et in terra pax*. It was at this instant that one of Mr Hitler's celebrated flying bombs exploded in the near neighbourhood . . . we simply went on singing; after all, it was just a part of life or death, depending on which way you chose to look at it. Still we were ignored by the Press.

An ongoing headache of those early days was where to hold the weekly rehearsals. It became desirable in every way that I should secure a church appointment, not only that it might serve as a rehearsal venue, but also that I might set about restoring my fast rusting organ technique. However, the war in Europe was over before, late in 1945, I made the acquaintance of the Reverend Cecil Clark, Vicar of Christ Church, Woburn Square.

We struck up an instant friendship based on a community of interests and ambitions. I was appointed his organist, my problems were solved, and many new opportunities became apparent. The Renaissance Singers began to broadcast with some frequency as well as appearing at Dame Myra Hess's Lunchtime Concerts at the National Gallery; but, with so much else now going on in London, audiences at our own concerts began to dwindle seriously and so, of course, did our balance at the bank.

Then, somehow, the seriousness of our affairs came to the notice of Peter Pears, and he offered to give his services to what was to be our forthcoming recital of Music for the Feast of Christmas. A programme was built around him and the choir and my good friend Ralph Downes joined us as organ accompanist. Once again Marylebone Church was packed to the galleries, the Press were present and generous in their reports, and we were saved. Furthermore, both Pears and Britten began to take an interest in my future schemes, offering both advice and suggestions and, in the case of Pears, a willingness to participate. I continued with severity to concentrate on the 'voicing' of the choir in terms of the music it performed, dismissing all the contraltos and replacing them with counter-tenors. And thus I met what I can only describe as the greatest eminence (not *gris* but for good) in the progress of my life: I refer to John Whitworth, born in Ely, just down from being a choral scholar under Boris Ord at King's, Cambridge, and who came to sing with the Renaissance Singers. I shall have much more to say relating to him in due course. Meanwhile I recall with pleasure how, after a performance of Tallis' *Lamentations* given at its correct pitch with all male voices, Our Music Critic of *The Times* wrote that the counter-tenors sounded like 'neither man, woman, nor child.'

Now the memories become truly vivid. Christmas would be the time and we always contrived to give our Christmas recital on the Saturday as nearly as possible preceding that Feast. With Marylebone Church well filled despite the cold, we would assemble plus string band and with Ralph Downes at the organ. A typical opening would be Purcell's 'Behold, I bring you glad tidings of great joy', with its spacious and dramatic introduction sung by that splendid bass, Alexander Henderson. Then, brisk and three beats to the bar, the music broke into joyous trio, the barque cavortings of the top line becoming, as it were, *trompette militaire* through the sheer virtuosity of John Whitworth's singing, while the strings played one down-bow followed by two up, in the authentic French manner insisted upon at the Chapel Royal by King Charles II. What a King was that man; he who had perforce spent so much of the Cromwell régime at the French Court, and had thus been inspired to establish his own band of 'twenty-four violins' (popularised without malice in the Nursery Rhyme 'Four and twenty Blackbirds') in

Whitehall. Woe betide the singer who made any mistake for, as Pepys informs us, it always 'made the King laugh.' And to hear the music sung thus and bowed thus was to create the illusion that one's feet were no longer on the ground!

The programme centre-piece would perhaps be a Nativity Mass by one of the Continental masters. Mediaeval carols might follow. The ending would almost certainly be Richard Dering's *Quem vidistis Pastores*, the strings doubling the voices of this joyful motet. But for me, with my choir in recess, Christmas was inevitably a flat episode, playing for the congregation at Woburn Square. One of my tenors wrote to me in his Christmas Card 'but you can imagine what I feel like at the Chapel Royal, once home of Blow and Purcell, while we roll out the inevitable anglican chant.'

During this time, Cecil Clark and I set up a scheme whereby for ten Sundays during each of the London University terms a full choral evensong was sung by a double choir of voices drawn from the Renaissance Singers, and was the first choir other than that of a cathedral to broadcast the weekday Evensong on the Home Service. Christ Church, Woburn Square no longer exists. It was not a particularly notable building, but gelled happily into the surroundings of that beautiful square and boasted a fine reredos by Burne-Jones. It was also excellent in its acoustics. I began here to put into practice my ideals in terms of being a cathedral organist. The Renaissance Singers also used it regularly as a venue for BBC broadcasts which, amongst other things, helped the church's own finances. It was in fact in this church that I first met Bishop Colin Dunlop, as well as many other notable people who came there to hear the music. But still I was nagged by many private and personal problems which caused me great but, had I but known it, needless embarrassment. The 'partner' of my late student days had long since gone. My mother had, for the time being, moved to Philbeach Gardens in order to supervise my housekeeping and the top floor tenants had departed. After repeated desertions and returns, I was legally advised to change the locks of my own front door and to refuse my 'partner' further admission. I was then to institute proceedings for divorce which, such was the nature of the law in those days, would take three years. But I lived in terror of her emerging somewhere in public and creating a dreadful scene. I told Cecil Clark all about this and he did his best to reassure me. But what effect was this (shameful?) business going to have upon my ambition for a cathedral appointment? I told Bishop Dunlop about it and he said that there need be no adverse effects provided that I did not marry again. The Church of England had no machinery for official annulment. He even knew of a Dean (of course, he mentioned no name) who was in the same position as myself.

Somewhere in Charing Cross Road I bought (at a ridiculously low price) a beautifully bound set of the three volumes of Boyce's *Cathedral Music*; also two sets of the Oxford Press *Tudor Church Music*, each set amounting to ten volumes. The Oxford Press could now find no market for such things, and the cost was negligible. From these, and from Jebb's collection of *Reformation Preces and Responses*, it was possible to set up the basis of the Christ Church, Woburn Square, repertoire in a manner more authentic than anything to be found in cathedral usage of that time. I was rapidly becoming well known and, in certain circles, unpopular. Alec Robertson, head of BBC Music Talks, invited me to speak on a number of occasions, and I always did this fearlessly, broadcasting my knowledge and opinions which I knew to be both sound and correct in their basis. As a Roman Catholic, I think Alec Robertson derived considerable enjoyment from the anger and prejudice which he knew that I must be stirring. It was no wonder that in my initial applications for any vacant posts occurring at cathedrals I was never short-listed, but always ignored.

Then one day I was asked to present myself for consideration for St Albans Cathedral. I was to take a full rehearsal of the choir, play for Evensong, and to be interviewed by the Dean. I thought how St Albans would suit me admirably, being fairly near London. I would still be able to keep on with the Renaissance Singers and so not disappear from central musical life. But the post, in perfectly fair competition, was given to Meredith Davies who, duly moving from there to Hereford, scandalised the Three Choirs Festival by including music by Webern in one of the programmes. He left Hereford to become a full-time orchestral conductor, earning a considerable reputation for his readings of contemporary music. For me, there was still Woburn Square and all that it was fighting for. Cecil Clark was certainly glad not to lose me.

The next rocking of the boat, and to this day I have no idea how it came about, was that the Dean of Liverpool Cathedral wished me to succeed his retiring choirmaster. He wrote to me saying he would be in London on a specified date and invited me to dine with him. Dean Dwelly proved to be an unfrightening and charming host, easy in conversation and unobtrusive in his assessing of myself. The evening ended with him inviting me to go to Liverpool, to see the cathedral and to hear the choir for myself, and to have some further talk. A date was fixed and I would stay at the Adelphi Hotel. By now he had seen that I was reasonably replenished with good wine and I fell in with these plans without much particular thought but, oddly enough, without any great feelings of enthusiasm. I did *not* like Liverpool; Gilbert Scott's cathedral I thought large and flamboyant to the greater glory of its architect and with little thought of Almighty God; the choir was *good* and the

organ monstrous; the Hotel like an extra-super Strand Palace, with the
dismal wailing of ships' hooters down in the Mersey Docks thrown in
for good measure. I returned to London hoping that I would never see
the place again.

Among those few people who had been, as it were, in the know, my
behaviour was such as to cause blank astonishment. That I should actually have 'turned down' the offer of a cathedral appointment was simply
beyond their comprehension; and indeed, if challenged, I would have
found it very hard to justify what I had done. I just knew within myself
that I had done the right thing. Cecil Clark was, of course, only too glad
to have me still with him. The broadsheets never now missed any of the
Renaissance Singers' concerts and press notices were consistently
glowing. *The Musical Times* featured me in a most effusive article,
complete with photograph. But on what did I think I was going to live?
Then, in the early spring of 1949, I was short-listed for Ely Cathedral.
My fellow competitors were Sidney Campbell of Wolverhampton Parish
Church and John Long, brother of the celebrated pianist Kathleen, who
was organist of Beverley Minster. Dean Blackburn wrote giving me the
time of a train that would get me to Ely in time for the morning Chapter
meeting. I was to stay at the Deanery for the rest of the weekend.

I duly arrived to be interviewed. 'Come into the Lions' Den,' said
the Dean kindly, and I was presented to Bishop Walsh who was the sub-
dean, Canon Ratcliff, the Ely Professor of Divinity in the University of
Cambridge, Canon Balmforth, Principal of Ely Theological College,
and the Canon Treasurer whose name escapes me. All of them greeted
me genially and I was invited to sit down. In so far as I can recall, I was
led into saying why I wanted a cathedral appointment and, apart from
it being a life-long ambition, I embarked on a vigorous diatribe regarding the inexcusable neglect of our heritage from Tudor times and that
following the Restoration. With the obsession and commitment of
youth, I did not spare them, but they all listened most politely.
Eventually I was dismissed and told that I might roam the Cathedral and
Close at my pleasure. Deanery lunch would be at the usual time, I could
attend the usual choir rehearsals and meet Dr Conway, talk with his
assistant, and be shown and allowed to play on the organ.

The Dean's daughter, Betty Blackburn, proved to be a welcome blast
of fresh air, so much so that I found myself telling her a faintly risky
musical anecdote at which she laughed uproariously in an excessively
'male' manner. The Dean's wife, addressing me benignly as 'young
man', asked me to meet her for tea in her (literally) withdrawing room
and 'to give an account of' myself. Conway sourly asked me what on
earth I wanted to come to Ely for, bedevilled with a lot of High Church
men. (This I found curious, for he had previously been organist of

Chichester with all its ritual and 'holy smoke'.) He said that I might sit with him in the organ loft during Evensong. The choir was awful and he was obviously tired of the whole thing. His assistant, a few years younger than myself, put himself out to be pleasant – but then he had to consider that were I to be appointed I would be entitled to replace him. He had no security of tenure. After a fascinating three days I returned to London and to wait. Long and Campbell had still to be interviewed. The days now dragged by interminably and in due course I began anxiously to watch the post. This brings me to an incident which I could wish never to have happened. I returned to my home late one afternoon to be asked by my mother what I proposed to do about earning a proper living. I said that just at this stage I was waiting to see whether I had been appointed to Ely. She replied 'Well you haven't', and handed me a letter with the Ely post mark which she had already opened. I know that I at once left the room, but I have no further memory of that awful day.

Christ Church, Woburn Square.
Choral Services during the Long Vacation & Michaelmas Term, 1948.

Sunday Services:
7.40 a.m. Matins.
8.0 a.m. Holy Communion
11.0 a.m. Morning Service.
6.30 p.m. Choral Evensong.

Music at Evensong.	Responses.	Service.	The Anthem.	The Hymn after the Grace.
TUESDAY, August 17th, at 3.0 *Broadcast Service*	Tho. Hunt and the Westminster use	Orlando Gibbons Short Service	O Jesu, Look George Kirbye	O most merciful (E.H.323) from "Munster Gesangbuch."
TUESDAY, St. Bartholomew August 24th, at 3.0 *Broadcast Service*	William Byrd Third Setting.	Michael Wise in F.	O how glorious art Thou Robert Whyte	Give me the wings of faith (E.H.197) Orlando Gibbons.
SUNDAY, Trinity XX October 10th, at 6.30	William Smith of Durham	Charles Wood in F (*Collegium Regale*)	This is my commandment Tho. Tallis.	Lord, in Thy name (E.H. 140) Ravenscroft Psalter.
SUNDAY, Eve of St. Luke October 17th, at 6.30	Orlando Gibbons and the Westminster use.	Tho. Walmisley in D minor	Blessed is he that considereth Michael Wise	O God of Bethel (E.H. 447) Henry Purcell.
SUNDAY, Trinity XXII October 24th, at 6.30 *Men's Voices*	Ascribed to Tho. Tallis	Adrian Batten Short Service	O give thanks unto the Lord Tho. Tomkins	O God of truth (E.H. 449) Scottish Psalter
SUNDAY, Eve of All Saints October 31st, at 6.30	William Byrd Third Setting.	Michael Howard in D.	O Quam Gloriosum William Byrd	O Gladsome Light (E.H.269) Louis Bourgeois.
SUNDAY, Remembrance Day November 7th, at 6.30	Tho. Tallis First Setting.	William Child in F. minor.	Justorum animae William Byrd	Strong Son of God (E.H.483) Orlando Gibbons
SUNDAY, Trinity XXV November 14th, at 6.30	Orlando Gibbons and the Westminster use	William Byrd Third Service	Almighty and everlasting God Orlando Gibbons	That day of wrath (E.H. 487) Tho. Campion
SUNDAY, The next before Advent November 21st, at 6.30	Tho. Hunt and the Westminster use	John Goss in E	Call to remembrance Johnathan Battishill	Jesu, grant me this (E.H. 413) Orlando Gibbons
SUNDAY, Advent I November 28th, at 6.30	Tho. Tallis First Setting	Osbert Parsley in G minor	Hosanna to the Son of David Tho. Weelkes	Behold the Bridegroom cometh (E.H. 3) Tho. Tallis

CECIL CLARK, *Vicar.*
MICHAEL HOWARD, *Organist & Choirmaster*

Chapter VIII

Ludgrove and Freelance Life

It was Dr Sidney Campbell who had been appointed to Ely. For me, it was clearly going to be life on the rocks unless I took drastic steps. So I arranged to go and be interviewed by the equivalent of Evelyn Waugh's *Church and Gargoyle*, scholastic agents, as he depicts them in *Decline and Fall*. They were encouraging and helpful in every way and I was shortly requested to go to meet Mr A.T. Barber, joint headmaster of Ludgrove. Mr Barber was in all senses a gentleman and furthermore, as a cricketer, had captained both Oxford and Yorkshire. My duties would be to teach the piano to a not very great number of boys, take three sing-song classes each week, play on a single manual hand-blown organ for the Sunday morning service, and to play a hymn on the dining hall piano at evening prayers. I would take my meals with the school and accommodation would be provided. A Tuesday absence to rehearse the Renaissance Singers need present no problem, nor need occasional absence for concerts or broadcasts. Although the headmaster had no ear for music, he saw that these things were of importance to me. It was arranged that I should start my duties in September. The music room with its small piano was for my own use at all times other than evening supper which I would take with three other masters.

As I recall, I liked Alan Barber and it seemed that my feelings were reciprocated. I suppose that the relationship must have been based on what Hieronymus Bosch would have described as 'a conjunction of opposites'. I changed the 'sing-song' sessions by substituting Folk Songs with the pictorial accompaniments of Benjamin Britten and Sea Shanties as arranged by Richard Terry. This did not meet with his approval, but the boys found my choice stimulating. I used my own gramophone records to promote elementary musical appreciation – Mendelssohn's 'Fingal's Cave' Overture, Beethoven's Fourth Symphony, Walton's 'Belshazzar's Feast'. He could not see how 'the very young' would possibly benefit from anything so serious! But when I instituted a short and voluntary Sunday evening listening session, several boys and one or two of the staff came back for more. I selected certain boys to form a chapel choir and so to lead the singing. This involved special rehearsal three mornings each week before school. They prepared two special carols – Wood's *Mater ora filium* and Warlock's 'The Five Lesser Joys of Mary' – for the Christmas Carol Service. Mr Barber came to me the next day, saying, 'I confess that many of us were rather disappointed in your carol service. We have always looked on it as an occasion when we all have a jolly good sing.' Then, through the machinations of Felix Aprahamian, I was asked to play the organ part in a performance at the Albert Hall of Beethoven's *Missa Solemnis*, with the London Philharmonic Orchestra and Chorus conducted by Victor de Sabata. This would involve two days absence from Ludgrove, and I approached Alan Barber with some trepidation. 'But of course you must do it, my dear fellow. Why, to be asked to play at the Albert Hall is like being asked to play at Lord's!'

So I spent nearly three more or less happy years at Ludgrove, realising how fortunate I was to be able to maintain all my work with the Renaissance Singers – and during this time I met John Whitworth and began to share solo recitals with him, in which I would accompany him on either the organ or the harpsichord. I recall how we gave a midwinter recital in the Jubilee Hall in Aldeburgh, as it were to keep the Festival pot boiling, and how extraordinarily well attended it was. In fact, work of this kind gradually became so pressing that my interests in Ludgrove started seriously to lapse to an unacceptable degree, and I left there just before the Easter of 1952.

Being thrown once again entirely on the insecure life of a freelance musician of specialised substance, I went to share diggings in the same house as John Whitworth in some rather seedy part of north London, but with organ practice facilities at a Church in Queen's Square, Bloomsbury. John having a car, we were able to get about as and when necessary. The rest of my time was spent in reviving my abilities as an organ soloist and working with the Singers. It was during this period that the Renaissance Singers commercially recorded the three Mass settings by William Byrd for Argo. Although I was not aware of it, this was apparently a pioneer enterprise and certainly led to recording engagements that were to come about in the future.

Then came my first visit to Paris. John Whitworth, whose French was fluent, had some personal connections there and, through them, contact with the British Ambassador. We were invited jointly to give a recital in the Embassy Church and also to broadcast a programme on Radio Diffusion Française. All music was to be by English composers.

I recall how it was a damp and drizzling morning as we set off in the bus from Cromwell Road which was to take us to Hounslow airport. It was my first experience of flying and the prospect filled me with no enthusiasm. But sadly, the Southern Railway was no more and the *Maid of Kent* had been blown to smithereens during the Dunkirk evacuations. It was not that I was troubled by air sickness; rather it was that the whole concept of flying seemed to be deliberately one of flying in the face of nature. I had always supposed that it was the speed of a plane creating pressure under its wings that lifted it from the ground and enabled it to 'float'. But it would seem that this was quite incorrect, and that a plane flies because it is sucked upwards by a partial vacuum over the wings. All the engines do is to make sure that it travels fast enough to create this vacuum. Well, I wasn't sick, but I was very glad when we came safely down at Orly airport. Although I have done much flying since then, it is *not* my favourite mode of transport.

We had been placed in the Hotel Angleterre, Rue de Londres, close to the Gare-Saint-Lazare. Opposite was a small café where the food and drink, after the rationing of England, seemed like a gourmet's paradise; and the prices unexpectedly reasonable! But for the main part we were liberally entertained and made much of, by a people who but a few years before had endured frightening hardships and dangers on their own doorsteps. Above all, I had never imagined that a great city could be so invigorating and beautiful, with anything that one might need 'just around the corner'. I suppose that Wren must have had something of this nature in mind with his plans for the rebuilding of London following the Great Fire; but of course the English, with imagination as damp as their climate, weren't having anything of that!

Our first engagement was the broadcast for Radio Diffusion, which was to be transmitted from the Chapel of L'Institute des Jeunes Aveugles. It was here that Louis Vierne had received his early training, first as a 'cellist and pianist, subsequently as an organist. The chapel was a fine reverberant building in the grand style of Baron Haussmann's Paris, the organ an instrument very much in the manner of Cavaillé-Coll, its voicing true, its mechanisms simple. Our programme was of the solo counter-tenor anthems 'O Lord, rebuke me not' by John Weldon and Maurice Greene's 'Acquaint thyself with God', and I played John Blow's *Voluntary for a Double Organ* and a magnificent virtuoso *Voluntary* of the same ilk by Henry Purcell.

As opposed to the BBC's meticulous and frequently irritating set up of Producer, Studio Manager, audition staff in the 'fish tank', green lights and red lights, everything here was of basic simplicity. A pleasant and very active man with excellent English made sure that I was 'at home' with the instrument, listened carefully while I played some extracts, then having adjusted and repositioned a couple of microphones rushed away to a listening room while I repeated the parts which I had already played. After this, we went through the same procedure while I accompanied John Whitworth. Eventually he settled himself wearing headphones at a table beside the organ console, saying that he would hand-signal to us when to begin each item. The programme was, of course, being broadcast 'live'. What the listener heard was actually happening . . . a very different story from our present-day system of push-button, tape editing, safety first broadcasting with the script-reading announcer safely divorced from the proceedings which, in any case, would all have taken place some weeks earlier. (With this in mind, I have always insisted that my CD organ recordings shall be of a through performance; if anything goes wrong, we return to the beginning.)

After the broadcast the Producer came to congratulate us and I then realised who he was – Gaston Litaize – an internationally renowned organ recitalist. He had been blind from birth.

Our recital in the Embassy Chapel was an expansion of the same programme, again with a beautifully voiced organ for me to play and to accompany. There was a fine reception afterwards and my meagre French was stretched to its limits – but John was always there to come to my aid. As to the women – their clothes – their perfumes – their manicures and nylon stockings . . . most certainly *Vive la France*! If I was drunk, I did not need any wine to make me so. And the climate, sharp – dry – it was beyond compare.

On the Sunday afternoon we were escorted to Notre-Dame to meet M le Comte de Saint-Martin, the *Titulaire* and successor to Louis Vierne, and to attend Vespers with him up in the west tribune while he supplied the necessary interpolations on Cavaillé-Coll's wonderful *Grand Orgue* (an instrument now destroyed, together with the liturgy which it once enhanced). M le Comte was urbane and courteous, carrying a tall silver-headed cane; his hat was broad-brimmed and floppy. Far below and far away in the choir, the Canons were already chanting their way through the psalms, for the (improvised) organ commentaries did not begin until the singing of the Office Hymn and Magnificat. The little *orgue de choeur* (seemingly virtually in another building) gave an appropriate back-drop to the singing of the clergy. One heard the rustle of mechanism as de Saint-Martin drew the various stops and set the *Jeux de combinations* which he would require. The console telephone croaked like an expiring frog with a message from the sanctuary advising him of pitch . . . and then it began. Verse by verse the *Grand Orgue* replied, sometimes like a pool of water, sometimes in a thunder of ecstasy that had the whole building shouting in echoing reply; and then at the end, and after Benediction, came the *Sortie*. To every man his instrument; to every dog his day; the thrill of it all is with me still. Did Vatican II really know what it was doing when (as it were) it muzzled the Holy Ghost? And Cavaillé-Coll's masterpiece has been long destroyed.

And so it was back to England; back to Hounslow Heath where bold Turpin had once stopped the Bishop's coach; back to Cromwell Road. For John, back to singing at Westminster Abbey and for me, back to an ever increasing bill for unpaid rent. (It was, of course, my aunt Nora in her ever self-effacing saintliness who eventually 'bailed me out'.)

Then the news broke that the Octagon of Ely Cathedral was riddled with death-watch beetle and an enormous sum would have to be raised in order to have this eradicated. Dean Blackburn had retired and the Dean was now the Very Reverend C. Patrick Hankey.

John Whitworth, more or less of an age with myself, had been born in Ely at a time when the population of this cathedral city was only some eight thousand. Himself educated at Kimbolton, he gained a choral scholarship to King's College, Cambridge. The fulfilment of this was delayed by the war during which he served in the RAF. On coming down from the University, he became a lay vicar at Westminster Abbey under Dr (later Sir) William McKie until 1971. He was the true counter-tenor of his time as opposed to the more falsetto qualities of Alfred Deller, and in London formed a group of ex-King's choral scholars known as the *Regale Singers*. It was while listening in the 'fish tank' to one of their broadcasts from the Maida Vale Concert Hall-Studio that I first met Boris Ord. Much of the music sung had been specially arranged by John himself.

I am not sure what connection if any John Whitworth had with the Hankey family, but early in 1953 he wrote to the Dean's wife suggesting that he and I should give a shared recital in the cathedral, the proceeds of which (small though they would be) would go to the appeal which had been launched to save the Ely Octagon. Be that as it may, the offer was accepted and a date agreed for the forthcoming June. I can even give the date of that particular weekend in that the psalms for Evensong on the Friday evening were those for the tenth evening. For some reason, the words and the accompanying chant of Psalm 53: 'The foolish body hath said in his heart: there is no God,' became engraved on my memory, even as they are today.

Once again I found myself staying at the Deanery, but in a very different atmosphere. The Dean, benign, tall (he was well over six feet), as spare in figure as a heron, cultured and easy in conversation. 'Some people don't like Breugel,' he said, standing beneath a picture overhanging the drawingroom fireplace. 'They seem to think he has a lavatory mind. Perhaps I've got a lavatory mind myself!' Mrs Hankey was small, comfortable and with a quick wit. She made reference to the unveiling of a statue of Queen Victoria at which she had been present –

the Queen sitting on some sort of flat stone seat and leaning slightly forward, 'exactly as if she were about to reach back for the toilet roll.' They were both determined in seeing that we should feel completely at ease. Dr Campbell arrived in a bustle of pleasantry in time to drink a cup of tea. Here I was, face to face with the man who had done me out of a job. Nevertheless, I asked him if I might come up into the organ loft during Evensong and was welcomed to do so. The Dean's Verger arrived, complete with poker, to conduct the Dean to the cathedral. Campbell talked to me with an almost neurotic enthusiasm. The Canticles were sung to the 'High Service' by Richard Farrant. Times were arranged when I could practise and when we could rehearse.

That evening, when the cathedral had been closed at seven o'clock, I was taken over to make my first practical acquaintance with the organ – a vast and amorphous 1908 instrument by Harrissons of Durham. Seated at the console, I found that not only was there a lag from the pneumatic action, but also an acoustic lag as the sound travelled from the triforium across the choir vaulting. That which one heard in no way coincided with the movement of one's hands. I saw at once that John Whitworth was going to have to sing from the organ loft if there was to be any liaison whatsoever between us. The principal works in our programme were the Bach alto solo Cantata no. 53: *Schlage doch* and the second of the three Organ Sonatas by Hindemith. I seem to remember that John also sang the superb counter-tenor solo anthem: 'O Lord rebuke me not in thine indignation' by John Weldon.

The recital took place on the next day after Evensong. There had been more Tudor and Restoration music sung at the services, and when the concert was over we repaired to the Deanery to have tea and to prepare for departure. Standing outside by the car door I duly thanked the Dean and his wife for their hospitality, and added that for me the occasion had provided a marvellous feast of my favourite choral music. The Dean said that as far as he was concerned there could never be too much Tudor music. I replied, 'How fortunate Dr Campbell is to have a Dean like yourself.' Then, taking a last look at that wonderful church, all green and grey in the evening sun, I got into the car and John drove us away. I never expected to see it again.

Chapter IX

Cathedralis Eliensis

'God moves in a mysterious way His wonders to perform.' I was not only familiar with Cowper's hymn, but also with J.F. Roxburgh's devastating analysis of its mixture of metaphors. 'If his "designs" are "treasured up" they are presumably not put into practice. How then does he "work his sovereign will"?'[8] Among my ecclesiastical books I had, and still have, Martin Hurlimann's superb collection of photographs of English cathedrals. I had bought it, according to the fly leaf, in 1950 and it still falls open easily at the collection of plates showing Ely.

But I seemed to have lost faith, resigned to a career as a musician working in a purely secular manner. In a sense, the Ely recital had exacerbated former pain. Thoroughly depressed, I felt that my fortunes had now sunk very low. Since my appointment at Ludgrove I had given up watching the press for any collegiate position that might have become vacant. Then, after some ten days in this slough of despond, I received a letter.

It was from the Dean of Ely to say that I might or might not know that Dr Campbell was leaving the cathedral at the end of July, and in case I should be interested he presumed to enclose details of the post of organist. At about the same time, John Whitworth had a letter from Sydney Campbell asking whether or not I was still hoping for a cathedral appointment or had I, by now, lost interest. I, of course, wrote 'promptly yet carefully' to the Dean making a formal application and giving the names of Bishop Dunlop and Arthur Hutchings (Professor of Music at Durham University) as references. Sydney asked John was there some matrimonial difficulty in the background? Had there been a divorce?

Without loss of time, I went down to Ely to see Sydney and to explain my circumstances. He retired to his telephone and then told me to go over to the Deanery where I was expected. I was received with warmth and kindness and asked just what the trouble was. Floundering, I did my best to explain the exact situation. To my surprise and immediate comfort the Dean simply said 'I think the Church has managed to deal successfully with far greater problems than that in its time.' He added that, by great good fortune, he and I would appear to have identical ideas on the subject of liturgical music and that he now proposed to discuss the matter in Chapter. I would hear from him in due course. The Chapter comprised the very men whom I had met four years previously – Bishop Walsh, Canons Ratcliff and Balmforth, and the Treasurer. I was overcome by indescribable relief.

Waiting, I kept my mouth shut; the prospect was too good to be true. But in what was probably a comparatively short stretch of time *the* letter did arrive. 'Agreed in Chapter this day ... that Mr Michael Howard, Director of the Renaissance Singers, be appointed Organist and Magister Choristarum in our Cathedral ...'. A contract was enclosed for my signature together with a copy for my own keeping. The appointment was to begin as from 1st September 1953 at a salary of £400 per annum; a house would be made available to me in the College, rent and rates free; my duties would be to be responsible for the music sung in the Cathedral and for the training of the choristers and lay clerks according to the existing programme; there would be an assistant organist whose appointment I would confirm and who would carry out such duties in support as I might require. Services would be sung by the lay clerks alone in the fortnights following Christmas and Easter and all services during the month of August would be 'plain' – i.e. said.

My aunt Nora was absolutely delighted by the news which had by now been reported in the Press. She, having retired from Bedford High School, had recently bought a house in Framlingham in Suffolk, where she and my mother had gone to live. After all, not so very far from Ely – I would be able to visit them. For the sum of £10 I bought a 1928 Morris Oxford Empire model drop-head; the removable windows being of ancient and cracked perspex; the head lamps dipped literally by a back-breaking lever to the right hand side of the driver; the crash gear change being in the centre and operating from a gate-change that was set inside-out, i.e. first forward was nearest to the driver, and so on. There was, of course, a bulb horn and also an electric horn that would put most light-houses to shame. The tyres could be removed, the steering locked, and the vehicle thus run on standard gauge railway track! Cruising speed was probably about thirty-five to forty mph. The registration was MM, but I do not recall the number. Boris Ord always referred to her as 'that yellow wagon'. I fear that my aunt Nora did not approve, and never rode in her! Just beyond the great gateway, Ely Porta, were a set of garages converted from old stables. One was made available to me and it was there that 'Emma' was kept.

Of the sixteen choristers and eight singing men, four of the boys were probationers and the men included one supernumerary. The Head chorister at that time was a boy called Howard Thomas. He put himself out to do everything that lay in his power to make my initial life easy. During late July I had, at Sydney's invitation, played for a weekday Evensong (Wood in C minor and Gibbons' 'Almighty and everlasting God') and had been introduced to the lay clerks. My first acquaintance with the boys was in the third week of September. Up to then the services had been sung by the men only. This meant that for the psalmody, Te Deum and Benedictus we used the plainsong psalter of Briggs and Frere. Every day I scrupulously corrected the books so that the chants respected the proper *Flexes*, complete *Mediations* and correct *Finals*, just as I had corrected the books for use at Christ Church, Woburn Square. When, slightly before the end of this initial period, the Dean returned from his holidays, I found him waiting at the foot of the organ loft stairs. He had come to say that he had never before realised that English plainsong chanting could be so beautiful and so dignified. At the last of this, my initial set of plainsong Evensongs, I found a man with a very small boy wandering apparently lost under the Octagon. Suspecting a new chorister and his father, I said that I could take them over to the choir school after Evensong and suggested that they should come up into the loft while I played for the service. I can still see the man sitting on a chair with his tiny and obviously terrified son on his knee. That boy was none other than Bill Jeremiah, and the wonderful singing boy that he eventually became is preserved for ever in our famous record, *Music for the Feast of Christmas*, which he concludes with his performance of *The Coventry Carol*.

To my surprise, I had found that I was not going to live in the house that had been occupied by Sydney Campbell and had by tradition been the organist's house. That was now to become the home of Sir Will and Lady Spens, he being Steward to the Chapter. I was to occupy the Almonry which was at present being got ready and decorated against my moving in during the forthcoming January. I was told that it was a most exciting house, the ground floor being a vaulted undercroft five feet below ground level, and the other two floors included two bathrooms and no less than seven bedrooms! In the meantime I was given a large and comfortable room on the top floor of the Deanery and was to be looked after by a Mrs Bagshaw, an old friend of the Hankey family, who also had a flat in the Deanery. I was given a set of the necessary keys and was at liberty to come and go as I pleased. So my domestic existence proceeded comfortably up to and including Christmas.

The next thing, apart from drawing up the fortnightly music lists for the printer, was to come face to face in the practice room with my choristers. They, like myself, obviously wondered what they were in for, but when they discovered that my attitude was simply that of being another one of themselves (except that I was *primus inter pares*) we rapidly became good friends bound together by a common goal. The real problems that faced me at this stage were twofold: their tone and style of production when heard in the practice room was unacceptably thin and screechy; the repertoire, apart from a fair amount of Tudor and a small amount of Restoration music, was of that faceless type that presumed to call itself contemporary but was really scarcely worth the paper on which it was printed; and there were great holes when it came to the best of traditional cathedral music of the eighteenth and nineteenth centuries. Ralph Downes' parting words to me had been *festine lente*, but this was more than I could stand and in any case the two problems were interlocked.

I talked to the lay clerks about the matter, using as much discretion as I could muster and backing what I had to say with the compliments that their singing of plainsong had already aroused. They listened with patience, accepting the fact that my schemes were going to involve a severe cutting back of the existing repertoire, and tacitly conveying that they would co-operate with me in all that I intended to do. Some of them had been singing in that cathedral for many years and had already experienced many 'sea-changes'; and in any case I suspect that they thought that all organists were more or less mad. I was scrupulous in addressing them collectively as 'Gentlemen', but later I came to know most of them individually as good friends. One thing they would not stand was pomposity, but fortunately such was not my nature.

The Dean was less happy and feared that the lay clerks would become bored and slack, even though I assured him that I had discussed the matter with them fully and would seem to have won their support. I explained that the choristers' voices required to be totally 'revoiced' and that time could therefore not be spared in rehearsing quantities of music which, in any case, I would have intended ultimately to discard. He was further worried when I told him that it would probably be the summer of the following year before the choir would be properly revoiced as a true entity.

He certainly did not expect the inevitable apparent degeneration that appeared to take place during the first three months, and at Christmas said 'it was better under Sydney'. But it was from Howard Thomas that the far-seeing support came. 'Before Mr Howard was appointed, we used to sing like girls. Now it is going in the right direction.'

It was to my friend and (at that time) working colleague John Whitworth that I turned for guidance. My aim was singing boys with a range up to C in alt and then down through a rich head voice and across the lower break to the G below middle C. In other words, voices that were virtually an upward transposition of the true counter-tenor. But I needed knowledgeable help and direction in how this was to be achieved. John explained to me the essential techniques of breathing on a firmly supported base, the development of diaphragm control, the imperatives of relaxed arms and shoulders, jaws and neck, looseness of mouth and comfortable resonance in the head. He also came down to Ely on more than one occasion to listen and to discuss, going on afterwards to stay with his mother who had by now moved to Hemingford Abbots.

I shall never forget the unquestioning trust with which those choristers responded to me from the very beginning. Based on my talks with John Whitworth, each practice began not with music but with a carefully programmed series of exercises incorporating all the vital physical points upon which to base their eventual singing.

The time required to do this meant a drastically cut repertoire and enabled me to get rid of an amount of the undesirable music which they would, in any case, associate with their former ways. Furthermore, the physical exercises were susceptible of being made almost into the fun of a party game. I recall the Dean unexpectedly walking into a rehearsal just as we had got as far as loose neck and jaw technique. In this the boys hung their heads forward and shook them while emitting a bubbling groan through slack lips. I think he must have concluded, like so many a lay clerk, that all organists were basically mad. Politely we stopped, but he just said 'Don't take any notice of me,' – so we continued with our daily routine. Shortly afterwards he departed, probably filled with grave doubt. He had not heard a note of music!

Naturally, before it was possible in any way to build, what had been previously there had to be broken down to its foundations. However much I might try to explain, it was inevitable that the Dean should think that I was merely ruining all Sydney Campbell's work of the previous four years – which, in a way, I was – and hence his remark of harsh criticism after my first Christmas. He must have been excessively worried. But with the resumption of choral services after the short Christmas break slight signs of a new 'voicing' began to appear. At the same time I moved into the Almonry, gloriously romantic and bitterly cold. In the February I developed bronchitis. I went to John Whitworth's new flat in Kensington, was supervised by the local doctor and, after three weeks, checked through the Brompton Chest Hospital. During my absence my assistant organist had had unimpeded care of the choir and services and, not knowing of the specialised methods on which I had been working, everything came to a standstill.

But boys do not forget easily provided the break is not too long and, upon my return, we got down to work with an increased intensity. By the end of Holy Week the Dean felt able to say to me, 'Your Good Friday music was better than it has ever been before.' The relief was beyond description, and I also felt reasonably sure that come the summer there was going to be a choir really worth hearing.

And so it transpired. We were now beginning to be able to expand the musical repertoire with some of the works from the enormous list that I had in my mind, the whole choir was beginning to respond as a single instrument, and when one day both Sydney Campbell and Marmaduke Conway appeared at a service, I was in no way ashamed. By now the choristers were producing a wonderful, full and relaxed tone, with dynamic control through their entire range from a floated *pianissimo* to a lambent *forte*, all of which was reflected in those lines sung by the lay clerks, and all with perfect intonation. One day a Catholic friend of mine, James Phelan, sat with me during Evensong. Afterwards he said, 'I was amazed. I could hear and understand every word of this evening's psalms – and you must remember that until today I had never heard them sung in any language other than Latin.' In due course I related his remarks to the choir, and indeed there *was* something special about Ely psalmody. Our chant book was a fine manuscript collection peculiar to ourselves. The psalms had all been 'pointed' by Dr Conway, showing a wonderfully sensitive appreciation of Coverdale's language (as fine literature as any ever produced by an Englishman).

At the end of July 1954 came the annual choral recess and all Cathedral services would be said until the re-assembly of myself and the lay clerks at the beginning of September. I had already been thinking of a holiday in France, if only to get away from England's steaming heat, and I was particularly anxious to see the wonders of Chartres Cathedral and the miracles of its glass. Canon Balmforth was a great Francophile and urged me to carry my plans further. The Chartres glass he agreed was incredible; but there was so much of it that it was almost impossible to appreciate its true magnificence and its sheer quantity tended to make the whole building strangely opaque. By all means go to Chartres, but the finest glass of all was surely to be found in the cathedral of Bourges, some forty miles south of Orleans and the Loire. Here the glass was set spaced between plain windows and so showed to far greater effect while leaving the church itself pleasingly illumined. Furthermore there was a fantastic West Front while within, the building was apsidal – vaulted throughout and with unbroken double aisles.

Fired with all the enthusiasm of a young man but thirty years of age, I began to make my plans. My passport was in order but the amount of money that one might take out of the country was strictly limited – as was the amount of money that I had available. I bought a nylon shirt (daily washable and able to be dried overnight) and a light weight back-pack into which I put spare socks, pants and handkerchiefs. Night wear I rightly considered to be superfluous. I booked through on the Newhaven–Dieppe steamer and then intended to hitchhike or walk or whatever else might come my way. My limited French I had improved a little through reading.

My first and almost the only mistake that I made was on disembarkation at Dieppe. Feeling hungry after three hours on the sea, I went to a café and ordered an *Omelette aux fines herbes* together with roll and butter and a demi-carafe of red wine. But when I called for *l'addition* I got a shock! Then I remembered that Dieppe, being a sea-port town, the newly-arrived were regarded as fair game. However, it was a beautiful omelette; so, feeling restored and also with that delicious feeling of being 'abroad', I started making enquiries for the lorry or *camion* depot with a view to getting on the road to Rouen. I was soon told that there was, in fact, a sort of railway or tramway that plied between Dieppe and Rouen and that it was cheap. Joining this pretty basic mode of transport I was in Rouen by the early evening and found myself wandering down the famous *Rue de L'Horloge* looking for a likely room for the night. 'Good old Flaubert', I mused, having only recently read (in French) his *Madame Bovary* – and I recalled furthermore that Marcel Dupré had been born in this town and that Widor had given the opening recital on the magnificent *Grand Orgue* which Cavaillé-Coll had built for the Church of Saint-Ouen.

I found a bed, the price was negligible. I slept wonderfully through a night punctuated only by the sonorous clanging of the great *Horloge*. In the morning, having washed and made use of the sand-pit affair that the French are pleased to describe as a *toilette*, I emerged in search of real coffee, petit pain and butter, and then proceeded to take a look at the town. It was a painful sight: devastation everywhere and only the north transept of the cathedral intact.

Gradually I emerged upon the area where the *camion* drivers commenced their various journeys and soon found a man who was setting off across *La Beauce* as the great central plain is called. He was not going as far as Chartres, but could take me a very considerable part of the way.

I soon found that there was an unspoken etiquette among the French – an etiquette which could be frighteningly class conscious and yet was totally classless. When we stopped for food, one of us would pay for the meal and the other for the wine – rough red stuff that was served in litre bottles. One simply pushed down the cork with one's fingers and quaffed from the neck. In no time one had sweated it all away in that wonderful dry heat and was always ready for more. In no way was there any question of inebriation. When my driver put me down we solemnly shook hands and with a cry of 'Bon Voyage' he drove away. I reckoned that I was within long walking distance from Chartres and so, adjusting my back-pack, set out to tramp it.

The distance was much more than I had calculated and by evening I was tired and aching, but could see the great cathedral floodlit on the horizon. Turning into a field, sweating and exhausted, I lay down to sleep. The next thing I knew was that it was 'black bat night', the cathedral flood lights had been turned off, and I was bitterly cold.

Shift myself how I would, there was no more sleep for me that night and in the early morning I trekked along to the railway station and found an hotel at the bottom of the main hill leading up to the cathedral. But I was too tired to care about that for the moment. Booking in at the hotel I went to bed and to sleep.

I awoke in the afternoon and, having shaved, began to make my way up the hill that led to the cathedral. Half-way, I discovered a splendid café where I stopped for a badly needed meal including rare steak, *pommes frittes*, and a demi-carafe of *vin rouge*. I then continued towards the cathedral but paused for a few moments before a wall against which a whole lot of French de Gaulists had been lined up and shot by the Germans. The exterior of the cathedral, with its two unmatching West End towers and its flying buttressed surround, was magnificent. On entering, I became aware of two things: beautifully vaulted nave and aisles illusively lit by windows creating a strange sort of blue and white light; and Americans. Bit by bit my eyes adjusted, but I could see what Canon Balmforth had meant by too much of a good thing. Visually it was like a sort of indigestion and one would need months to begin to assimilate it truly. Eventually I asked a kindly verger if I might be allowed to see the console of the *Grand Orgue* which hung encased on the south wall of the nave, explaining that I was the organist of Ely Cathedral. He said that he regretted that it was absolutely forbidden and that the *titulaire* was away on holiday.

The next day being Sunday, I attended the cathedral for *Grande Messe*. Here was another manifestation of the Latin race. The cathedral was crammed and, to one side of the sanctuary, there stood a priest bawling the *Missa de Angelis* into a microphone which he held in one hand, while conducting a lethargic and unresponsive congregation with the other. In the background, the *orgue de choeur* played softly as if in shame. By contrast, I went in the afternoon to the beautiful church of Saint-Pierre where I found a priest seated at a small organ and accompanying himself as he sang Vespers. There was no one else in the building but it felt full of the presence of Almighty God.

On the next day I set off again on my great journey across *La Beauce*, getting occasional short *camion* lifts on the way and lunching at a small village with its inevitable superb church. By nightfall I was in Orleans glimpsing briefly the ghastly cathedral and seeking a bed. But the Loire! – at this point rock-bestrewn so that one could literally walk through its cool waters from one side to the other. It was here, sitting on one of these stones that I ate my supper of crisp roll and cheese, liberally washed down with good *vin rouge*. The next day I was lucky – a *camion* driver – going to Bourges, some forty miles south, and happy to take me.

My *camion* friend advised me to go to the Post Office where there was also a café and ask there about a bed. The café food was excellent, the wine was excellent, and yes, they did have a bedroom on the top floor with running cold water and the usual sandpit *toilette* just along the corridor. The food was cheap, the wine even more so, and the rent for the room a mere bagatelle. I calculated that at this rate I would be able to stay in Bourges for about five days while still leaving enough money to spare for my return journey. Then to the cathedral.

It was all and more that Canon Balmforth had led me to expect, certainly the most beautiful French church that I have ever seen. Its proportions seemed to be absolutely perfect and, of course, the glass being widely spaced stood out in a manner that was the antithesis of Chartres. I cannot understand why Henry James in his 'Little Tour in France' should have slanged it so. Furthermore, it adjoined a great garden of (to me) strange flora and fauna, all baking in the sun and dry heat. There were no vulgar hordes of chattering tourists but both cathedral and garden seemed to be places of interminable peace . . . though I am sure that the cathedral would be amply attended on both Sundays and Holy Days. Silence prevailed. I noticed that the *Grand Orgue* had been dismantled from the west wall and taken away, presumably for cleaning and restoration.

It suddenly struck me: what a strange country, so naughty, so wicked, so mercenary, so religious, and yet so artistic and inartistic. Was this the paradox that so charmed those of us who came from damp and proper 'keep your feet off the grass' England?

Alas the time came when I must return – a journey without particular event except the inevitable being swindled over something at Dieppe. And so to Ely, well-nourished in every sense, to prepare for the recommencement of my cathedral duties with the lay clerks at the beginning of September.

So far the BBC had left us alone, but we now began to take our place in the rota of Wednesday Evensong broadcasts on the Home Service. The following autumn (1955) saw the start of that most fruitful combination of the cathedral choristers and the Gentlemen of the Renaissance Singers both in broadcast and public recitals. Our Music Critic of *The*

Times was no longer making puzzled remarks about counter-tenors – 'neither man, woman, nor child' – but paying the most generous of compliments to the Ely choristers. One former such wrote to me in 1998 of the qualities which they felt always to have been imbued in them: 'preparation, style, excellence, fairness, artistry, team work.' It is a letter which will always be preserved among my personal papers.

I now entered into that period of my life which I can only describe as my 'Elysian days'. There had never been anything like it before. There has never been anything like it since. The whole essence of collegiate worship is that it inevitably carries on, its sole purpose being the greater glory of God. Such members of the public who may have chosen to attend services did so, in fact, by courtesy of the Dean and Chapter. Ely has its own Parish Church and, in those days, there was also another church of Anglo-Catholic persuasion. In mid-winter, a weekday Evensong was more often than not sung in all its irresistible beauty in a building where, apart from the organist and choir, only the Dean, the Canons and minor canons, and the Vergers were present. The Bedesman who had rung the five-minute bell before service would be sitting at his table somewhere in the nave. The doors would be open to non-existent visitors but, by law, the Dean and Chapter were entitled to close the entire building to the public at any time.

In my time, the population of the city had risen to some ten thousand. There were no pretty 'ye olde' tea shops. Agricultural machinery was the main concern, sugar beet from the Fens the chief industry. Even the railway station – London, Cambridge, Ely, King's Lynn – was in the fields adjacent to the town. There was one particularly excellent grocers shop and a good butcher; a cinema and a (weekly) market held in a great square in the centre of the city; two hotels, of which The Lamb had obviously been the chief Coaching Inn; the usual other basic amenities and some fine houses facing the green to the west of the cathedral itself; a street, known as The Gallery, which combined with the nineteenth-century buildings of the Theological College; the Cathedral Close and its great Gateway, locked at ten o'clock every night and subject to the care of a night-watchman. Life was beautiful and tough. Once each year the market place became the scene of the annual fair – the Tawdry Fair, by derivation: Tawdry, St Audrey, St Etheldreda, foundress of the original Benedictine monastery. Thus, the blue and white rosette worn by the head chorister was known as a Tawdry; the Abbot of Ely, being also a bishop, the choir sides were (and remain) reversed, Decani being on the north; the market place annually filled with galloping horses, chairoplanes, bumping cars, cheap stalls, candy floss! Eastward, the brewery – Ely Ales.

Each afternoon I would go to have tea with the Dean and then leave (sometimes in his company, escorted by a verger) for the practice room in order to put the choristers through their vocal paces before Evensong. There was an unspoken, yet implied preciousness to every service as if it had never happened before and might never happen again. There were great jokes and great occasions. Every St Peter's Day we sang Byrd's setting of *Tu es Petrus – 'et super hanc petram aedificabo . . .'*. Among the boys the Dean was always affectionately referred to as 'super Hanc'. On Christmas Day the choristers had a snack lunch, and Christmas Dinner was served in the main school hall after Evensong. Dr Wynn, the then Bishop, and myself took opposite ends of the long table. Through everything I wanted for the good of the choir I had the support of William Brown, the Headmaster – all too soon from my point of view to leave and become Headmaster of Bedford. The Bishop treated me with great friendliness. Alas, all too soon he was to die and be replaced by someone of very different calibre.

A cathedral close is truly a strange place and not just the convenient picture of awkwardness as drawn by Trollope in his Barchester novels. All these people were so good and kind to me; yet the Dean and Chapter had no liking for the Bishop, while Brown (who was a vital cog in the wheel) was regarded as being of no significance whatsoever. No wonder that he was leaving that which he had made into so fine a school.

As to cathedral close characters, in certain respects I suppose that we did veer towards Barchester. During my whole tenure of office at Ely, I never met Canon Balmforth's wife – as indeed was the case with most of the residents of the close. It was simply accepted that she was of an hypochondriacal disposition and spent her days in virtual isolation, bespread upon a chaise-longue. One evening Lady Spens invited me, in company with several others, to join her for sherry. I now forget the context, but Canon Balmforth's name was mentioned. Lady Spens stiffened perceptibly. 'Yes,' she exclaimed, 'I had to call on the Canon this afternoon to return some papers. By mischance, I was ushered into the presence of his wife, so I cut my visit short. But as I was leaving, the good lady thanked me so much for praying for her. Well!' with raised eyebrows, 'I wasn't aware that I had been praying for her – unless I'd included her with Jews, Turks and Infidels.'

Our repertoire by now began to parallel Sam Weller's knowledge of London; it was 'both extensive and peculiar'. We were singing all the great Tudor Canticle settings with the exception of Byrd's 'Great Service' for which our choir did not have the required numerical capacity; also well known and little known anthems, both 'verse' and 'full'. Our Restoration music was now similarly complete and included such things as John Blow's 'dorian' service (tonally astringent and an obvious gesture to Tallis' work of the same title) and his superb 'Salvator mundi' which particularly appealed to the Dean. Gaps in the Purcell repertoire (extensive) were filled in and works by Pelham Humphries, Michael Wise, and others were added. Proceeding towards the eighteenth century brought Child's sombre and beautiful Canticles in E minor and a vigorous setting in A major by Elvey. Much Boyce was brought to light again and (it was an *in* joke) we always sang Battishill's 'O Lord look down from heaven' on St Swithin's Day!

The nineteenth century I enriched by the best of Walmisley, Sterndale Bennett, Wesley and Goss, including Wesley's magnificent service in E major. From the twentieth century, music by Vaughan Williams, Warlock and Britten took its place, including V.W.'s superb 'Coronation' Te Deum in F. Also there was much plainsong including the daily Proper Office Hymns, and those parts of the Mass which might be sung in the original Greek or Latin. Among the more recherché pieces were Cornyshe's devastating setting of Skelton's poem 'Woefully arrayed' – always sung on Good Friday – and hitherto unknown works by Tye and Taverner (who was so nearly imprisoned by Cardinal Wolsey). On *Red Letter* Saints' Days, a Sung Eucharist was sung to plainsong by the boys alone; Christmas Term residence was extended to include the Feasts of St Stephen, St John, and Holy Innocents. No chorister would willingly have exchanged his cathedral Christmas for a domestic one at home. Holiday began in their minds only after the Evensong for The Innocents. This Evensong was peculiarly their own. No lay clerks attended; Psalms, Canticles were unaccompanied plainchant, the anthem, the Coventry Carol in its original form.

Then, and most appropriately for me, there was 29th September – the Feast of St Michael and All Angels, with Dering's setting of *Factum est silentium*. And from the hanging mists of silence came the boom as of a great drum – DUM *comitteret bellum* – war was declared. DRRAACO roared the Dragon in utter futility as he presumed to do battle with the Archangel . . . only to find himself reduced 'alleluia, alleluia' to a very Reluctant Dragon indeed. The story in itself makes for fine high drama in its mere telling. But enhanced by Richard Dering's music it became devastating. To and fro Decani and Cantoris would hurl the protagonists until, utterly crushed, the poor Dragon had to retire with his tail between his legs. 'Alleluia, alleluia,' this was no suavely sung anthem, and after Evensong there would be a happy and hungry gleam in many an eye – not least among the clergy!

I will not pretend that the Almonry, as a residence, did not weigh heavily upon me. In description so romantic and picturesque, in winter it was a bitter and totally impracticable proposition to one in my circumstances. I obtained permission from the Dean and Chapter to sub-let part of it to my assistant organist who had recently married. This disposed of several rooms and one of the bathrooms. For a short time David Waddams,[9] a former chorister and graduate from King's, Cambridge, had the use of some other rooms before moving with his family to a house in The Gallery. He had joined the Cathedral choir as Cantoris alto, combined with the senior maths-mastership at the King's School. With another King's School appointment combined, Roger Firkins – a former Westminster Abbey chorister and a choral scholar at King's, Cambridge, became my Decani tenor. As an entity, the cathedral choir became something of a phenomenon. Every few weeks Boris Ord would attend Evensong sitting under the Octagon, having first of all been driven over from Cambridge in my 'yellow wagon' – would chat with the choristers afterwards and, to me, impart many words of wisdom on our journey back to Cambridge.

During my years at Ely, I was privileged to create a band of cathedral choristers without peer in this country. (I do not, of course, include Boris Ord of King's College, Cambridge or George Malcolm of Westminster Cathedral in this summary statement.) Apart from their daily rehearsals and their onerous duties in the cathedral, my choristers also combined with the male voices of the Renaissance Singers in both Third Programme broadcasts and in public recitals in London and elsewhere. Their BBC recording of Palestrina's *Missa Assumpta est Maria* was regarded as something extraordinary, for it was broadcast no less than four times on the Third Programme and then, for a fifth time, on the Home Service.

I instituted an annual early summer sequence of concerts in the magnificent Parish Church at Framlingham. The Ely choristers would be brought over by coach to sing the opening Evensong and to give at least one recital, and a programme would be played by a guest organist on the famous old Thamar organ, its pipework dating from 1674, its beautifully decorated case from 1630. On one occasion a chamber concert programme included Benjamin Britten's cantata *Abraham and Isaac*, hitherto always sung by contralto and tenor with piano accompaniment. For this I got John Whitworth to sing the part of Isaac, it seeming to me to be more apt that the character of a man should be sung by a man. Britten himself was present and was most complimentary. It is of course pure surmise on my part, but it was 1960 that saw the first of his operas with a part specifically written for counter-tenor: *A Midsummer Night's Dream*, produced at the Aldeburgh Festival. I wonder if we could have sown the seeds of inspiration?

In 1957 we were invited to sing at the King's Lynn Festival – Palestrina's *Missa Papae Marcelli* and the Duruflé *Requiem* with its fiendish organ part so brilliantly managed by Arthur Wills. During the concert interval I was invited to the Rectory garden to take champagne and to be presented to Queen Elizabeth the Queen Mother. When it came to the time to return to the church, we all stood aside according to protocol. But Her Majesty turned to me and said 'But Mr Howard, you must go first. Without you we are lost.' And after the concert she came and asked to be personally introduced to each and every one of those singing boys.

Returning to Ely, I invited various people to come to my house for drinks – and I had previously gained permission for my four senior choristers also to attend, provided that they drank no alcohol and were back in school by ten o'clock. All went well and at the time of departure three of the boys bid us good-night: but not so Bill Jeremiah. He said that it would not matter if he stayed for another ten minutes or so. I pointed out that I had an obligation on his behalf and that if he remained with us he would be ignored. He said everything would be quite all right; he would simply climb into school through the downstairs lavatory window. Stay he did; ignored he was; soon he decided to depart. And so back to school, where poor Jeremiah proceeded to climb in through the downstairs lavatory window, only to find his housemaster using the place for a more orthodox purpose! Thankfully I managed to avert the beating he was due to receive.

Meanwhile success followed success, culminating in 1958 with our gramophone LP *Music for the Feast of Christmas* which, combined with many rarities, includes John Whitworth's superb singing of Gibbons' *This is the Record of John*. Decca Eclipse ECS660, it ran into three editions and has become a collector's piece.

So we progressed from practice to practice and from service to service. So precious was it all that it was a case of 'Live this day as if thy last'. But it was also the most tremendous fun. Daily psalm practice: 'If he do but touch the hills, they shall smoke.' 'Players please,' I would shout, to the dislocation of all that we were doing. Or in the summer heat, and if everything was well in hand, I would turn up with a great bag of toffees, hand it to the head boy, and say: 'Clear off, the lot of you, and make yourselves sick. See you at Evensong.'

Nor was the fun all on one side. Once, some thirty-five minutes into a midday rehearsal, there was an ear-splitting jangle from inside the grand piano. I sat in silence. They watched in silence. The noise stopped. I still sat in silence. More tensely they watched in silence. 'Right,' I said, 'it seems as if lunch is early today. Get out, the lot of you, and take your dreary alarm clock with you.' Thus I left the room. But they knew, and they knew that I knew, that they would never, ever let me down. Alas, to my everlasting sorrow, it was the reverse that was to be the case.

It was from this band of choristers that came many persons of distinction. As musicians, James Bowman and Nigel Perrin, celebrated counter-tenors; Paul Ives, a 'cellist and County Music Advisor to Shropshire; Bill Ives, *Informator Choristarum*, Magdelen College, Oxford; many others, noteworthy in their various professions. Meanwhile, many girls of that generation have gone on to become wives and mothers, or, as single ladies, have achieved distinction in their own suitably chosen professions. And as to those who presume to say that they can hear no difference between boys and girls singing in choir, the answer must be that the boys are being very badly trained. Here I am bound to add that the boys of Boris Ord and George Malcolm, together with my own boys at Ely, sang the way they did because they were scrupulously 'voiced' to the acoustics of the buildings in which they sang – a feat impossible to the vocal abilities of small girls.

At Ely our 'quire' was stone vaulted (it had originally been the sanctuary) but its natural resonance was muffled by the wood of the high canopied stalls that ran along either side. To anyone sitting further west than under the Octagon, both singing and organ tones rapidly became distant and indistinct. This of course was why, even for singing in 'quire', the voices of both men and boys had to be fully developed and capable of extremes in range and volume. King's, Cambridge, because of its unbroken-throughout fan vaulting, required only the faintest of steady sounds at one end for it to be distinctly heard at the other. Both places demanded absolute perfection of diction. Westminster Cathedral however was an entirely different proposition, as George Malcolm was quick to recognise. Vast and domed with much hard reflecting marble surface, it was not conceived in terms of English Cathedral Music, but of music of the Latin Roman Rite. The repertoire was one of Palestrina, Victoria, Lassus, together with quantities of Gregorian chant and music ranging up to the twentieth century. The *instrument* or choir that was to perform it must be as correct both to music and building as are stringed instruments to a string quartet. Ely choir would have certainly sounded both ludicrous and unbearable in King's Chapel; the Westminster choir to be fighting against every disadvantage in the 'quire' of Ely Cathedral.

And by natural law, to rid ourselves of, or in any way to impede the experience of the traditional cathedral chorister, is to endanger the future of those voices which evolve from it: the counter-tenor, the tenor, and the bass lay-clerk voice, together with that depth of knowledge which they bring to their highly specialised calling. It must be obvious to the meanest ear that no contralto can match the counter-tenor in either range or vocal timbre, and traditional cathedral music was composed with a specific vocal quality and range in mind. The 'orchestration' cannot be changed without disaster and detriment all round.

But the winter months! – cold it was, and colder it seemed to get. Even in bed, with an electric fire burning all night, I seemed to be able to find no warmth. One night, a friend calling to see me, I took my keys and returned from the Lady Chapel with two rush-bottomed chairs. They made a glorious blaze for some twenty or so minutes, after which we perforce retired to the bar of the Lamb Hotel. Yet I must suffer it, for the thought of life without my cathedral was insupportable. My aunt Nora died, talking on her death-bed of what a fine thing it was that I should be at Ely. On analysis, it was really to her that I owed everything worthwhile in my life; yet I had never really even liked her, such was the introversion of my nature. A year or so later saw the death of my mother but her funeral did not take place until some twelve months after, for she had left her body to Addenbrooke's Hospital in nearby Cambridge. I attended her funeral and burial in Cambridge cemetery, returned to Ely to play for Evensong, and spent the evening seeking distraction in the bar of the Lamb Hotel.

A newly-appointed Precentor and his wife did their utmost to help me, making an arrangement whereby I should have at least one good meal each day, he being always prepared to listen to me while I talked, talked, trying to find the solution to an insoluble problem. Why was it that I was so intractable – simply not prepared to accept that the conjunction of opposites was an impossibility? The answer was that, except as a musician, I was simply not grown up; I was not adult.

Both Ted Longford and Joan showed incredible patience in dealing with me for, musical matters apart, I was becoming more and more an impossible person. The night Anna, my Samoyed bitch, died I telephoned Ted to say that I was distracted – I just did not know what to do. Within minutes he was with me and set about digging a good deep grave in the Almonry rose-garden. Then he returned to me, we wrapped Anna in a large blanket and, together, took her out and laid her to rest. Afterwards he produced a bottle of Beaujolais, told me to get two glasses, and stayed with me until I had managed to quieten down. Saying 'good-night', I went to bed and slept until dawn roused me the next day and all the birds were singing.

But his help was by no means confined to the domestic. I found myself in ugly trouble with the Cambridge police for urinating in a shop doorway. Of course the matter had to be reported in the local papers, but it was Ted who contrived to see that the wording was so ambiguous that it did not *have* to point to me.

I began consistently to take more and more refuge in drink, shamelessly quarrelling with Ted, always self-convinced that I was successfully covering my tracks. The Dean sent for me and in all kindness asked me did I feel I had a drink problem. I assured him that no such problem existed – and I truly thought I was telling the truth. I was in absolute control of all that I did. Cunning, baffling, powerful and a master of the waiting game I, of course had no inkling of the true nature of my enemy. I merely drank, perhaps on occasion, in order to relax. Little did I realise that I was on the brink of being lost. Further embarrassing and humiliating episodes came about, but I could always find what I considered to be reasonable and convincing explanations. I knew in my heart and as a fact that the Church of England had no machinery for the annulment of marriage and that in the service of Ely I must be a loner. But again in my heart I was childish enough not to be able to accept this ecclesiastical ruling and was ever seeking a way of jumping the reality of the situation. Loneliness and the inspired self-pity of alcohol obliterated all remnants of my sanity and drove me into the impossible position of living a double life. In the end, in the July of 1958, when everything was musically and liturgically at its height, I could stand the stress and strain no longer and, smashing my secret relationship on the one hand, I also tendered my resignation to the cathedral chapter. In doing this I incurred the Dean's grave displeasure. 'You have let us all down very badly,' was his dry comment. But I also think that I broke his heart.

The author recording César Franck

The Royal Academy of Music

Brompton Oratory

Right: St Peter's,
   Eaton Square

Below: The Chancel,
   St Peter's,
   Eaton Square

The organ, Tewkesbury Abbey

Right: Christ Church,
        Woburn Square

Below: The organ,
        Christ Church,
        Woburn Square

Left: The Choir,
Ely Cathedral

Below: Ely Cathedral

The organ, Framlingham Church

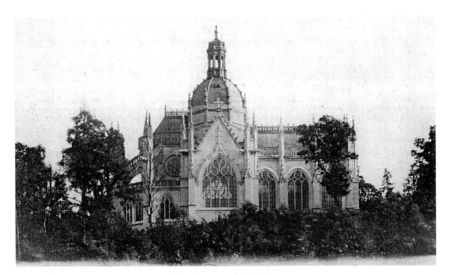

Farnborough Abbey

Christ Church, St Leonards

CATHEDRAL CHURCH OF ELY

MARCH, 1957

9 SATURDAY
7.40 Mattins
8.0 Holy Communion (Bishop West's Chapel)
5.0 EVENSONG. Responses—*Smith*
  Wesley in E.
  Cast me not away—*Wesley*
  Office Hymn 66

10 FIRST SUNDAY IN LENT
8.0 Holy Communion (High Altar)
8.15 Litany
10.30 MATTINS. Responses—*Smith*
  Benedicite: *Purcell* in B flat
  Benedictus: Chant—*Attwood*
  O Saviour of the world—*Goss*   Hymn 74
  Preacher: The Revd. Canon H. Saunders, Canon in Residence
11.30 SUNG EUCHARIST
  Kyrie: Orbis Factor—*Tye*
  Plainsong   Proper 676
  Hymn 330, pt. 2
3.45 EVENSONG. Responses—*Smith*
  O Jesu look—*Kyrbe*
  Wesley (to five voices)
  In jejunio et fletu—*Tallis*
  Office Hymn 66

11 MONDAY
7.40 Mattins
8.0 Holy Communion (Bishop Alcock's Chapel)
5.0 EVENSONG. Responses—*Hunt*
  Harris in A minor
  O Lord give Thy Holy Spirit—*Tallis*
  Office Hymn 66

12 TUESDAY
St. Gregory the Great, Bishop
7.40 Mattins
8.0 Holy Communion (St. Edmund's Chapel)
5.0 EVENSONG. (Sung by Ely Theological College)
  Magnificat—Tone IV
  Plainsong   Nunc Dimittis—Tune III
  Office Hymn 66   Hymn 421

13 WEDNESDAY Ember Day
7.40 Mattins and Litany
8.0 Holy Communion (Bishop West's Chapel)
4.0 EVENSONG. Responses—*Gibbons*. (Broadcast Service)
  Walmisley in D minor
  Wash me throughly—*Wesley*
  Office Hymn 66

14 THURSDAY
7.40 Mattins
8.0 Holy Communion (St. Etheldreda's Chapel)
5.0 EVENSONG. Responses—*Gibbons*
  Wood in C minor
  O that I knew where I might find him—*Sterndale Bennett*
  Office Hymn 66

15 FRIDAY Ember Day
7.40 Mattins and Litany
8.0 Holy Communion (St. Catherine's Chapel)
5.0 EVENSONG. Responses—*Byrd*
  Hunt (Short Service)
  Almighty and Everlasting God—*Gibbons*
  Office Hymn 66

16 SATURDAY Ember Day
7.40 Mattins
8.0 Holy Communion (Bishop West's Chapel)
5.0 EVENSONG. Responses—*Smith*
  Travers in F
  Hear my prayer O Lord—*Batten*
  Office Hymn 65

C. PATRICK HANKEY, M.A., *Dean.*   EDWARD DE T. W. LONGFORD, M.A., *Precentor and Sacrist.*

MARCH, 1957

17 SECOND SUNDAY IN LENT
St. Patrick, Bishop
8.0 Litany
8.15 Holy Communion (High Altar)
10.30 MATTINS. Responses—*Smith*
  Benedicite: *Lloyd* in B flat
  Benedictus: Chant—*Conway*
  Thou knowest Lord. *Purcell*   Hymn 73
  Preacher: The Revd. Canon F. N. Robathan, Canon in Residence
11.30 SUNG EUCHARIST
  Kyrie: Leroy—*Taverner*
  Plainsong   Proper 677
  Teach me Thy way—*Fox*   Hymn 335
3.45 EVENSONG. Responses—*Smith*
  Child in E minor
  O where shall wisdom be found—*Boyce*
  Office Hymn 65

18 MONDAY
St. Edward, King and Martyr
7.40 Mattins
8.0 Holy Communion (Bishop Alcock's Chapel)
5.0 EVENSONG. Responses—*Hunt*
  Cooke in G
  O Lord the maker of all thing—*Mundy*
  Office Hymn 65

19 TUESDAY
7.40 Mattins
8.0 Holy Communion (St. Edmund's Chapel)
5.0 Evensong

20 WEDNESDAY
St. Cuthbert, Bishop of Lindisfarne
7.10 Mattins and Litany
8.0 Holy Communion (Bishop West's Chapel)
4.0 EVENSONG. Responses—*Byrd*. (Broadcast Service)
  Purcell in B flat
  Out of the deep—*Batten*
  Office Hymn 65

21 THURSDAY
St. Benedict, Abbot of Monte Cassino
7.40 Mattins
8.0 Holy Communion (St. Etheldreda's Chapel)
5.0 EVENSONG. Responses—*Gibbons*
  Kempton in B flat
  If we believe that Jesus died—*Goss*
  Office Hymn 65

22 FRIDAY
7.40 Mattins
8.0 Holy Communion (St. Catherine's Chapel)
5.0 EVENSONG. Responses—*Byrd*
  Gibbons (Short Service)
  Lord for Thy tender mercy's sake—*Hylton*
  Office Hymn 65

23 SATURDAY
7.40 Mattins
8.0 Holy Communion (Bishop West's Chapel)
5.0 EVENSONG. Responses—*Smith*
  King in F
  Blessed be the God and Father—*Wesley*
  Office Hymn 67

24 THIRD SUNDAY IN LENT
8.0 Litany
8.15 Holy Communion (High Altar)
10.30 MATTINS. Responses—*Smith*
  Benedicite: *Lloyd* in B flat
  Benedictus: Chant—*Walmisley*
  Comfort O Lord the soul of Thy servant—*Crotch*   Hymn 484
  Preacher: The Revd. G. R. Kemp, B.D., Director of Religious Education
11.30 SUNG EUCHARIST
  Wood (Phrygian)
  Kyrie: Traditional
  O taste and see—*Langham Williams*   Proper 678
  Hymn 304
3.45 EVENSONG. Responses—*Smith*
  Farrat (High Service)
  Hide not Thou Thy face—*Farrant*
  Office Hymn 67

MICHAEL HOWARD, *Organist.*

Chapter X

In the Wilderness
Cantores in Ecclesia

So then there were three. Henry Coleman, like myself an ex-Woodard man, had been organist of Peterborough Cathedral since 1921. After many years of mutual misery he divorced his wife and in 1944 married again. He was at once dismissed by the Dean and Chapter. Malcolm Courteney Boyle, born in Windsor Castle in 1902, was acting organist of St George's Chapel, Windsor, from 1924 until 1927 and in 1932 was appointed Organist of Chester Cathedral. He had divorced his wife when (as Arthur Hutchings put it) 'she allowed her dentist to give her more than gas.' But when he himself decided to marry again, the Dean and Chapter demanded his resignation. And now, myself. They both made headlines in the penny press. As far as I know I was ignored, but the news spread like wild fire. Meanwhile I resigned from the Renaissance Singers. So too did David Higham who had been for many years a member of the bass line and Chairman of the Committee, negotiating engagements and gramophone recordings, the last of these being the LP made in Arundel Cathedral of Palestrina's *Missa Aeterna Christi munera*. He was also to me a staunch supporter and friend and in his professional capacity he begged me to write my memoirs. But by now I was too confused and riddled with self-pity to be able to produce anything other than the obnoxiously tedious. The script has been destroyed.

I was invited to give weekly lectures on Music and Liturgy to the students at St Augustine's College in Canterbury. Here the nuts and bolts of the Church of England were already creaking – as it were, a formidable suggestion of things to come. Saturday morning was treated as being a Sunday, so that after the early Eucharist the young gentlemen could spend the weekend with their families or, at least in the case of one of them, go hunting. I think that they enjoyed my lectures, but it was obvious that they saw no relevance in them to their future lives as clergymen.

I also lectured and gave tuition in music at Battersea Polytechnic – now a 'university' based near Guildford. But more than anything I drank and was seldom sober. I could not stand, and was not prepared to make any effort to stand, the pain of reality. Little did I realise in my stupefaction the criminal pain that I had caused to my Ely choristers and the sadness I had brought to the lay clerks. It was to be many years before I appreciated fully the significance of this. George Malcolm wished me to succeed him at Westminster Cathedral, but this was refused because I was not a Catholic. Ralph Downes, with all the objectivity of true friendship, asked me to play for occasional services at Brompton Oratory.

I moved into a house in Church Square in Rye. Prompted by my pre-war memories of childhood and innocence I somehow thought that by my returning to those scenes I would find relief from all my troubles. I was of course playing the classic game of the captive alcoholic – for wherever I might choose to go I must, perforce, take myself with myself. My ever mounting debt of thousands of pounds to Lloyds Bank, my arrears to the Inland Revenue, every penny that I owed to anybody and anything – they were all still with me. But I still had the option of running up debts in Rye itself, opening an account with the Westminster Bank, leaving bills unpaid at various shops, and unpaid 'slates', as I made my steady progress from pub to pub. And above all it was vital that I should appear to be important and successful to my new neighbours.

That I was in fact in some degree 'successful' was true, for I frequently broadcast talks on musical matters for the BBC. But I was doing no playing – could, in my condition, do no playing – and I was doing no conducting of any importance. I professionally coached and trained a young boy of eight years so that he simultaneously was accepted for the choirs of Chichester and Winchester Cathedrals – leaving his parents to sort out the embarrassing impasse! Then one day my good friend, the late Basil Lam, telephoned me and suggested that we had an urgent discussion.

Basil – not for nothing did he have that formidable chin – could be very down to earth and cold blooded. I was guilty of sheer and inexcusable wastage. I had great gifts that were essentially peculiar to myself and I was selfishly withholding them and all that they might impart to the arts in general and in particular to the world of music. No one was going to feel sorry for me and, in fact, I was as good as forgotten already. If I would get down to it and form a first rate professional chamber choir, not only would he give it his personal support but would also see that the BBC music department became aware of what was on their doorstep. As to singers: advertise, audition, select, be without compromise; there were plenty of such who would rally to the call.

I made contact with Terry Edwards (later to become chorus master at Covent Garden Opera House) and a long-standing colleague, the counter-tenor Geoffrey Mitchell. Between us we set up astringent auditions in a goodly sized room adjoining the Little Oratory Chapel at Brompton. The Oratory Fathers – especially the, then, Prefect of Music – were helpful in every way. A pianist was engaged to play piano accompaniments. Our first intake included people like the soprano Felicity Palmer, my friend John Whitworth, James Bowman, the tenor Peter Hall, and basses of the calibre of Edwards himself, David Thomas, and others who would match and blend. In fact it was the story of the Renaissance Singers all over again except that this time it was at the highest professional level. It was carefully explained to each selected person that there could be no fee for the intense opening rehearsals, but that there was every reason to hope that properly paid engagements would soon be forthcoming. Everything would be arranged to suit their interests and deputies would be forbidden. The numbers would be six soprani, two mezzo voices, two counter-tenors, four tenors and four basses, two of the latter being able to sing fully and comfortably to the E below the bass stave.

I selected the name *Cantores in Ecclesia* as giving us free range through ecclesiastical music of any period and from any liturgy – but we began conventionally enough with music by Palestrina which I knew would fall within Basil Lam's remit at the BBC. Scrupulously I worked with the choir on absolute uniformity of vowel formation, resonant consonants (especially the ringing 'r'), full dynamic range, and the essential through voicing that would create them into a single and flexible instrument. The Corporation accepted us and we achieved our first broadcast.

Next we hired the South Bank Queen Elizabeth Hall for a public concert. Our programme there was of the Vespers by Iuan Cererols, an eighteenth-century Benedictine of Montserrat, and Monteverdi's six-part *Magnificat* from his Vespers of 1610, with the organ part superbly realised by Ralph Downes. A good audience ensured that we were not out of pocket and the Press were generous with their praise. What was this cunning automatism that was keeping me going? – for it now seemed that I could only achieve normality when my blood stream was well balanced with generous supplies of alcohol. Socially I kept myself more and more to myself.

A broadcast of music by Tallis won for us the Prix Musicale de Radio Brno and with it an extended concert tour of Czechoslovakia. This was during the Dubjek regime when the Russians appeared to have departed and the whole country was blossoming into a sadly false Spring. We were met at the airport by a Mr Novi who had served in England during the war, were each given a vast sum of money (which we would not, of course, be allowed to take out of the country), and told of our itinerary: concerts in Prague, Brno and Bratislava, and for me an interview on Prague Radio. I was told by the Producer that I was now in a Catholic country and might feel free to say anything I liked. The only sight of arms that I ever saw was the revolver carried by the janitor at the main entrance to the Radio Station. I talked without inhibition.

Then to the main rehearsal studio to hear the Czech Philharmonic rehearsing a Dvorak Symphony – playing with a fire and affection released after a too long imposed diet of Prokovief and Schostokovitch. Afterwards to the foyer of the Smetana Hall, to drink litres of creamy soft Czech Pils and to knock back by the thimbleful a Slivovitz which virtually made the scalp on one's head part from one's skull. We were housed in the immediate city suburbs – very post-war, basic and drab. Transport was by an excellently integrated system of tramways running at frequent intervals; private cars were almost non-existent, nearly everyone spoke excellent English, and we were treated with great affection. The food, not just because it was different, was delicious and smilingly served by black suited waiters ever anxious that one should be pleased, as they would hope to be pleased by one's music or when they went to the opera. The disease of 'pop-culture' had yet to contaminate this delightful country.

We had brought with us a large and interchangeable repertoire ranging from Byrd and Palestrina to Messiaen and Poulenc and, at the suggestion of Ralph Downes, his young New Zealand pupil Gillian Weir was with us to furnish accompaniments as and when required, and to perform as a solo item Hugh Wood's recently composed *Capriccio* – a thrilling virtuoso work in its own right. The first concert was to take place in the glorious Baroque Basilica of St James and a special rehearsal room was put at our disposal. Posters everywhere advertised the event and once again my mind was taken back to those end of the war days in London with the Renaissance Singers.

At this time in Czechoslovakia, if a concert was advertised for 8.00 p.m. or 9.00 p.m., that was the time the audiences started to arrive. We of course had assembled in the West Gallery well before and I was interested to note from the chairs, music stands and encased double basses that it was usual practice to have an orchestrally accompanied High Mass sung on Sundays – from the calender list, Mozart, Haydn, Schubert, Beethoven in C. Meanwhile the church began to fill . . . on and on until every chair was taken, people were sitting on the pulpit steps, on the sanctuary steps, on the floor and crammed standing in the aisles. Eventually we began to sing and it was disconcerting to find the degree to which the building had lost its resonance. I think that, for once, we were all slightly nervous in the face of such people's tremendous thirst for good music, and since it was all sacred music it was a natural part and parcel of their own religion.

Our next move was to Brno itself but I was disconcerted to find that we were to fly. The norm was intercity airbus, the steam-hauled railways being used for freight only. Furthermore, the planes themselves were both crude and noisy, as it were like being inside some sort of tumble dryer. Brno airport was simply a field with a strip of tarmac and generously populated by hares who took no notice of us or anything else. We reported at a sort of shed and from there were conveyed by coach to the outskirts of the city. Brno itself turned out to be a vast but properly planned pedestrian precinct with the tramway forming an external circle. The church where we were to perform showed at once how very literal an attitude the people adopted towards their Catholicism. For instance the High Altar, while carrying the mandatory six candlesticks, had as its centre-piece an enormous cross upon which hung the life-size body of a man (*Ecce homo*), his hands and feet cruelly pierced, his head drooped and his beardless mouth agape, utterly dead with that last cry 'He gave up the ghost'. It was shocking to behold, and intended to shock it was.

So on to Bratislava and the Danube (not blue, but the colour of mud), only some forty miles from Vienna. After the intensity of Brno the secularity of this town came as something of a relief. Great squares with the tramcars clattering and bucketing around and a vast hotel where we were to stay. It had obviously been the luxury hotel in 'the bad old days'. My bedroom on the first floor had been the ballroom, now completely denuded with no curtains and a single bed in the far corner. But the food was good and the Pils was good, as, of course, was the Slivovitz. We now had time in hand and a studio was made available for our daily rehearsals. The eventual concert was to be in a Concert Hall, beginning when the audience had decided it was the right time for them to assemble. But the applause! Never was such a sincere reward to a choir singing now not only as a single instrument but also responding to the slightest nuance.

All too soon it came to an end and there followed the (to me) dreadful air-hop back to Prague during which I was more than once convinced that we were going to crash. Then the emotional farewells, the returning of such money as we had not spent, and our flight back to dear old bloody old England. At Heathrow friends and relations were waiting to greet choir members and I was left to return home with my bottle of Slivovitz – but small comfort now. A few days later I was summoned to see Sir William Glock.

I had been responsible for a great service to the BBC and its music.

What reward did I want? Sir William's secretary sent for Basil Lam. Eventually, following considerable discussion, I suggested the complete Tallis/Byrd *Cantiones Sacrae* of 1575, but combined with suitable presentation this would run to five programmes. Glock's reaction was typical. 'Do it,' he said and subsequently the music was issued, with the essential sleeve essays, as an LP boxed set by Editions de L'Oiseau-Lyre. By then, the Russian tanks were back in Czechoslovakia.

Sir William Glock did not forget us. For five consecutive years we appeared at the Promenade Concerts as well as at the Cheltenham and Bath Festivals, also broadcasting Palestrina's *Canticum Canticorum* which, in its turn, was duly issued commercially by L'Oiseau-Lyre. By this time I fear that I was, ever aided and abetted by alcohol, beginning to get serious delusions of grandeur. The Russians successfully put an end to Prague Spring, but why not a *Rye* Spring Festival? I would call it Rye Spring Music in order to avoid confusion with the long established Rye Festival which took place annually in the autumn. And my venture would not be wide ranging as was the Rye Festival itself, but would concentrate on a major choral recital to be given by *Cantores*, one or two recitals of chamber music, and an exhibition of pictures at the Art Gallery. Thus, through this latter idea, I met and became friends with John Piper.

So a committee was formed, and guarantors set up against loss. But the more did the committee advise me to tread with caution, the less was I prepared to do so. Also, we did not take into account the fact that when the Festival proper took place, the town was full of German and American tourists; in the spring it was far too cold for there to be any visitors at all. That in the first year we more or less got away with it was partly due to the fact that John Piper's exhibition was a success in its own right and that the BBC recorded and broadcast the concert in which *Cantores* with the Haffner Chamber Orchestra (leader Trevor Williams) gave a splendid performance in the Parish Church of Haydn's *Missa Cellensis*. I have a pirated recording of this performance, and it was good.

After the third year, Spring Music overdraft stood at several thousand pounds. An emergency meeting was called at which I quarrelled violently with everyone and, losing my temper completely, walked out of the room and left them to clear up the mess. In spite of the evidence before my eyes, I was still capable of honestly self-deceiving myself that the correct procedure was to carry on and, given time, everything would adjust itself. As to the guarantors who were now liable, why had they guaranteed their money in the first place?

In the meantime, John Whitworth (who in no way was concerned with the above) and I continued our working partnership as and when occasion occurred. I recall how he shook Uppsala to the foundations with our recital there in the Dom, as the Cathedral is called. They had simply never before heard or ever imagined such a voice, with its trumpet-like quality and perfection of diction. Continuing our tour in Sweden we came to Linköping where our host was Baron Mannerheim. After our recital we were conducted to the Schloss which was the family home. The Baroness explained that part of the building was now closed off; they could only afford to live in the 'flies'. Nevertheless, the 'flies' successfully incorporated a fine music room with harpsichord, chamber organ, and a vast library of gramophone records. Before our evening meal we came upon the Baroness talking to two beautiful young Swedish lasses. Concluding her remarks she said, 'Don't be too late coming back'. 'Crikey,' exclaimed John Whitworth when they had left the room, 'what absolutely super girls.' 'Oh yes,' responded the Baroness with a smile, 'we do have very nice servants!'

We stayed up into the small hours, talking, myself being pestered to play Bach on the organ, and listening to recordings. It was on this night that I first heard Webern's *klangfarben* scoring of Bach's *Ricicare* from The Musical Offering. Also that night I slept between linen that was all beautifully monogrammed with the family arms.

It was no wonder that we were late the next morning and were still breakfasting and talking when we should have been boarding the train that was to take us to Stockholm. 'No matter,' said the Baron, and going to the telephone he had the Helsingborg–Stockholm boat-train express stopped for us. I can still see the vast black steaming locomotive with its train of luxurious carriages standing at the station and the Station Master, in his top hat, waiting to conduct us aboard . . . while the infuriated and exhausted passengers who had been travelling all night across Germany and Denmark watched in despair and displeasure. In no way is Sweden like that today, having become a 'peoples' country' where the lowest common denominator is the norm.

Through BBC broadcasts I made many new friends – among them the composer Martin Dalby, the 'cellist Eleanor Warren, and Hans Keller. At one such broadcast concert we sang Schubert's beautiful Mass in G major with string band accompaniment. William Mann, the no longer anonymous 'Our Music Critic' of *The Times*, said in his review that it was the finest performance he had ever heard in his life. Martin Dalby composed and dedicated to me a setting of the Mass which we performed at a BBC Invitation Concert with the brass parts played by the Philip Jones Brass Ensemble.

Another public concert, also broadcast, was of Listzt's *Missa Choralis* given in the church of the Benedictine Abbey in Ealing. This work is fraught with its own peculiar tonal difficulties. Not only is it full of enharmonic changes, but these are carried to such an extent that for much of the time the music is positively atonal; also the organ is used sporadically, so that any deviation in choral pitch means instant disaster. Small wonder that, although one of Listzt's masterpieces, it is but little known. We rehearsed in the early afternoon and the concert was in the evening. With my ever growing inclination to self-efface-ment I spent the intervening time in going to the cinema. What I saw, I do not know.

Next came another London appearance at the Queen Elizabeth Hall. For this I had chosen Bruckner's 'Wind Band' Mass in E minor in which *Cantores in Ecclesia* were accompanied by fifteen woodwind and brass players from the Royal Philharmonic Orchestra. Again the same sort of tuning challenge occurs. The second and first counter-tenor lines grad-ually build with a divided soprano line over the opening ten bars. They then continue *fortissimo* backed by the four horns. Absolute tuning is of the essence! After the concert one of the clarinettists came up to me and asked how did we do it? Like Beecham, I was giving nothing away. Here is another work most unjustifiably neglected, but perhaps one can begin to see why.

We were invited to sing at the Flanders Festival. Our last concert there was in the church of a Benedictine Abbey, when we sang the Victoria Four-part Requiem together with all the relevant plainsong omitted from the polyphonic sections. Strangely, in the circumstances, I can still remember this with absolute clarity; also, how deeply moved were so many of the monks. Back in Ghent after the concert I fell against a wall, cracking my skull and bursting my left ear drum. That I do not remember, but I do remember waking up in hospital and being in excru-ciating pain. It would seem that there was no question of being able to do anything immediately to alleviate my distress because of the high level of alcohol in my blood stream.

While considering myself to be perfectly sane, I now see with hind-sight that I was, in fact, raving mad. The next morning I discharged myself from the hospital and was put by the Festival Authorities into an hotel. This was just what I wanted for, though there was no abatement of my agony, I did know that I had a bottle of high proof whiskey in my suitcase. After about a week, a good friend who had stayed behind with me took me to the airport and accompanied me safely back to England. I had been indescribably fortunate still to be alive.

At home I was given constant medical attention, but it was many weeks indeed before the pain left my head and, *videte miraculum*, my hearing was restored to normal. In my weakness I began, little by little, once again to practise the organ. To my amazement, my musical memory did not seem to be impaired. The faults all lay in my attitudes and in this I found not only training and help, but in addition the most tremendous encouragement through extended discussions with my friend George Malcolm. He too had known virtually parallel experiences and was never ashamed to admit to it if by doing so he could possibly be of benefit to others. His obituary notice in the *Daily Telegraph* of 15th October 1997 makes this abundantly clear. We had all been seeking happiness by running away from reality, certainly, in my case, causing the most dreadful damage to innumerable other people. No wonder I had never grown up. For true happiness means facing reality and accepting it without morbidity and self-pity. Nothing could ever bring back Ely, but I could now assess the wonder of its true value in my life and thus build upon it for such future as might remain to me. I happen to have a disease that can attack in either mental, spiritual, or physical form, the one inevitably leading to the other; but with the help of powers greater than myself it can be kept at bay. Alcohol is poison to me in every one of my senses. Only a madman tries to live on poison!

Somehow I learned that Dean Patrick Hankey was living in retirement, a widower, in the Gatehouse of Dorchester Abbey in Oxfordshire. His son held a nearby living and was able frequently to be with him. With some trepidation I went with David Waddams to call upon him there. When we were announced by the housekeeper, he was sitting in an armchair reading. Being nearly blind, he was wearing an elaborate magnifying fixture with the book held before him on a stand. But when he rose to greet us, all my fears were dispelled. There he stood, as tall, as slim, and as reminiscent as a heron from the Fens, absolutely delighted to see us. Tea was served, and for me it was as if we were back as of former times in the Deanery at Ely. The only difference was his voice . . . a little weak and apt to split high when in mid-sentence. When we were leaving he insisted on coming out into the street where we were to catch our bus. Taking my hand in both of his, he blessed me and said how happy I had made him. He died soon afterwards.

(On my sitting room wall, facing me as I write, hangs an autographed silk screen print by John Piper. It shows the exterior of Dorchester Abbey church in all its splendour. Perhaps the most rewarding recital fee that I have ever received!)

One of the most poisonous things which I now had to face, and indeed I was given no chance to forget it, was that I owed Lloyds Bank in the Strand several thousand pounds and added to this I was in debt to the Inland Revenue for several hundred more. But I was given no opportunity to turn a blind eye. By almost every post increasingly menacing letters were arriving from one or the other of these institutions. I started to sell furniture – a beautiful antique desk, a valuable set of dining chairs, the most precious parts of my library including all those books of antiquarian value. But as the money came in to me I never seemed to bank it, but paid the cheques to the landlord of my local pub and simply used the proceeds to subsidise further drinking. If the alcohol level ever began to diminish in my blood stream I found myself sweating, shaking, and reduced to an hysterical state of terror. So I reached the ultimate; I decided to kill myself.

I considered (as I thought!) quite sanely the various options and eventually decided to slash my veins. I assumed that I would then lose consciousness and for ever know no more. I armed myself with razor blades and a good sharp meat knife but I felt that in the circumstances perhaps a little Dutch courage was justified. So I went to my local inn and, on the pretext of entertaining some people 'just down from London' collected two bottles of gin. I drank and stood considering the razor blades and the meat axe. I drank some more. By the time I had drunk a bottle and a half of gin I felt that I had better get started.

I don't know which came first – the fainting or the black out. At some point, I came to – shattered and shaking with fright, bruised all over, both my wrists lacerated – covered in blood.

A few days later a strange man came to see me. But instead of being sorry for *me* he told me about himself, and my reaction was to think 'I am glad I'm not like that' and to proceed to feel very sorry for him. Well, at least for a moment it stopped me from feeling sorry for myself! He asked me to go to a meeting with him where I would know nobody and nobody would know me. All that I needed to do was to sit quietly and try to listen . . . and, if possible, not drink any more alcohol before the day when he would call and take me in his car.

In fact, the recollection of my great suicide attempt so sickened and disgusted me that the very idea of ever touching alcohol again reduced me to a sort of paralytic revulsion. But my new friend told me that this was dangerous and might only be a temporary frame of mind. When I wished, I could always talk to him about the other troubles that were causing me to feel so valueless. But he did not offer me any financial aid. Rather, he suggested, it might be a good idea if I went and discussed my affairs willingly with my creditors. Of course, they were not going to 'let me off' but they might well be prepared to meet me halfway. Ignoring them would only land me in bankruptcy.

I was amazed at how reasonable normal people were prepared to be, once they saw that I sincerely wished to do my best; and after a year or so of scrimping and screwing on my part a distant relative died and I inherited a sum of money which made me solvent. I began to suspect that perhaps there *was* Somebody beyond my comprehension who wished to care for my well-being provided that I was willing to do my share of the work. I had free will. It was up to me. And up to this moment in time I have touched no more alcohol.

What it all amounted to was that an insidious and evil power far greater than myself had been inexorably destroying me. Gradually, but only gradually, without false pride and with the help of others of similar experience, I could now embark upon the most exciting and rewarding journey of my life, knowing that never would more be asked of me than I was capable of giving; but if I chose to take charge and try and rush, then I would create impediments. Look at how my keyboard technique once had to be developed so far before I could play *this* piece – and yet further developed before I could play *that*.

As a musician, perhaps the first miracle was this: it was a Sunday morning in the following summer and I was walking along Watchbell Street. As I drew near to the Franciscan church there, I heard ladies voices singing the Latin plainsong of the Mass. They were not perfect and their tuning was by no means perfect, yet it was utterly beautiful. By the time I reached the door of the church the Celebrant, a Franciscan Friar, had ascended to the pulpit. It was the time when there was still much unrest following the second Vatican Council. 'Please understand,' he was saying, 'Latin is the language of the Church.' I now forget how he continued but I and my Welsh border collie Dushkin stayed where we were until the end of Mass. In due course I approached him. It was characteristic of a Franciscan that he should first of all fondle Dushkin who, like any bitch, could take any amount of attention. He then asked us both to come into the clergy house and talk. A Brother brought us a pot of tea, and milk, sugar and biscuits.

I told him who I was, that I had once been a cathedral organist and how I had wrecked it all, about my secular travels and experiences, how I had nearly killed myself with drink, and how the beauty of the plainsong had attracted me to the church door. I asked him who trained the ladies singing from the west gallery and why there had been no organ accompaniment. He said that he did his best to train them but that if I would like to take it on there was a very nice harmonium in the gallery and that both I and Dushkin would be more than welcome. Choir practice was on Thursday evening, but there was no stipend available. His name was Edmund O'Gorman and he expected to be the priest in Rye for at least another three years. The fact that I was not a Catholic did not matter in the least.

It was one of the most wonderful moments in my life . . . I who had so nearly gone to the devil and who had presumed no longer to believe in miracles! The ladies were delighted and always gave Dushkin a Christmas box (squeakers, dog chocs and the like) after the Midnight Mass. While we had to keep the bulk of the chant simple for the sake of the congregation, I taught them how to breathe properly and to listen to their tuning, and we assembled a fine repertoire of the more elaborate plainsong settings of the *Kyrie Eleison*. I also grew to love the harmonium which was capable of great powers of expression, and would play elevation preludes and *sorties* by many of the French eighteenth-century masters. Father Edmund frequently invited me to take meals with him and, from time to time from some hidden source, would produce small amounts of cash to help me keep going.

Despite many a slip and slide on my part, things really did begin to get better. In one sense I was lucky over alcohol. I had never been interested in the taste of the stuff, but simply drank it for its effect. By now I decided that reality was infinitely to be preferred. Reality may not have been altogether fun, but whatever it was it never failed to be exciting. And I acquired the long-term tenancy of an upper maisonette in nearby St Leonards-on-Sea.

Two very important things emerged from this move. One was that I found in Justin Pryke, Dushkin's veterinary surgeon, a life-long friend. The other was gaining unlimited access to the organ of Christ Church in return for playing for Evensong and Benediction on Sundays. My ruined powers as an executant now began to be restored to me and the twice-weekly visits to Rye to maintain the singing at the Franciscan Church completed the balance. Trains were convenient, Rye being on the Ashford–Hastings link, and Dushkin was a phlegmatic traveller, while never failing to greet Father Edmund and the ladies of the choir with uninhibited squeals of joy. Indeed, she seemed to think that that beautiful church was her special domain and I am sure that St Francis would have agreed with her. After the Sunday Mass we would sometimes lunch with Father Edmund, but always finished by walking over the fields from Rye to Winchelsea Station picking up the train there for our return journey.

The domestic front became equally exciting and absorbing. In the rundown areas of St Leonard's I was able easily to acquire all that was necessary to my kitchen. I also found, at virtually no price to speak of, a genuine Pembroke table and four delightful Edwardian dining room chairs. Good bedding and linen was to be had from a shop in a road running down to the sea. I found an ancient Hoover which is still working efficiently today. I still had some pictures and engravings (notably of Ely Cathedral) and a fair quantity of books and music scores. A friend sold me a comfortable Parker Knoll armchair for £10 and finally I managed to buy a reliable 'on its last legs' car. It would not have passed today's MOT!

So life continued for some five or so progressive years. I was asked to give the opening recital on the newly restored organ in a neighbouring town. *Not* a happy 'restoration', but I played a full Bach programme from memory. Other engagements followed, notably at Arundel Cathedral. Then Father Edmund was transferred to Manchester and we were subjected to a series of 'supply' priests from Canterbury who insisted on using the vernacular. I left Rye altogether. There was nothing I could do to alleviate the distress of those devoted and faithful Catholics who were the parishioners there. Father Edmund kept in touch with me by correspondence. One day, my telephone rang.

The telephone call was from the Precentor of St Michael's Benedictine Abbey in Farnborough, Hampshire. The Prior had decided that the Abbey was in need of an organist of professional standing and he would be grateful if I could arrange to go and see him – being prepared to stay overnight and possibly even longer. I would be welcome to bring Dushkin with me. After a telephone conversation with Ralph Downes I arranged to do just this. Father Edmund (one needs to remember that Franciscan Friars are not an enclosed Order) warned me to keep my head with the 'Monkey Men', saying that monasteries might look all very peaceful and romantic from the outside but that it could be a startlingly different story once one got within their walls.

It is true that there was everything to cloud my judgement externally. The domed church itself had been built for the Empress Eugénie, widow of Napoleon III. The architect had been Gabriel Destailler and the style was that of 'gothique-flamboyant' – flying buttresses, water-sprouting gargoyles, bottle-glassed windows, stone vaulting. The vast crypt chapel below was a huge mausoleum where reposed the bodies of the Emperor, the Empress, and their son. Outside were the graves of the Empress' faithful man-servant and that of her dog. Nearby there was a hedged ground where lay the bodies of previous members of the Abbey community. The two wings of the community building were in the style of the Benedictine Abbey of Solesme; they were joined together by what had once been a large country house. The church itself contained what was, by now, England's only Cavaillé-Coll organ – an instrument which was to play an important part in my future life.

The Prior, the Very Reverend Dom David Higham OSB, and the Precentor invited myself and Dushkin to a comfortable office next to the Prior's own room or 'Cell'. Their object was to tell me precisely what the Abbey would require of me if I were considered suitable and should be attracted by the appointment. First, I would play for the Solemn Mass on Sundays and also for the Capitular Mass and for Vespers on weekdays. The latter services were at 8.00 a.m. and 5.00 p.m.; the Sunday Mass at 10.30 a.m. All music sung at Mass was in the Latin tongue – plainsong for the Proper, choral settings for the Sunday Ordinary. All else was vernacular. The organist was required to play or give a suitable improvisation during the *Offertorium* as well as providing a *Grande Sortie* at the end. The celebrant and altar party were fully robed, the servers wearing white gloves, and everything was carried out in a leisurely and dignified manner. (Curiously enough, there was no sanctus bell; perhaps something peculiar to this particular Order?) Plainsong was accompanied except during Advent and Lent, or at a Requiem when everything was unaccompanied and the organ silent throughout.

There was no choir school. Boys were recruited by word of mouth and were then auditioned. There were some ten or twelve men (unpaid amateurs) providing alto, tenor and bass. Their ability to read music was not high. The boys had two practices each week – Wednesdays and Fridays. So also did the men but the Friday practice was intended for the full choir. Boys had to be ferried to their homes but there was some help available to deal with this. The organ was free to the organist for his own practice at all times during the day when Offices were not being recited; also, since it could not be heard in the monastic buildings, at any time during the night. The appointed organist would have his own tastefully furnished room with heating supplied. He might bring any necessary books and pictures of his own. He would take his meals with the community but at a table separate from them. The doors were locked at 9.00 p.m. each night so notice must be given of any late *exeat*. A fortnight's leave would be granted after Christmas and after Easter and the month of August would be regarded as time for holiday. The honorarium would be £800 per annum, payable quarterly in advance. The Abbey grounds were extensive and would be splendid for exercising Dushkin. Indeed, the place was so enclosed that one might have been in the depths of the country.

The upshot was that I stayed for a week, attending all services and all functions. I was then told that from the point of view of the Community the matter would be discussed in Chapter. I myself would obviously be glad to go away and think carefully through my own reactions. We would make contact in due course and, if necessary, they would write to Ralph Downes and George Malcolm for references.

On returning to St Leonards my own thinking took me back to certain episodes which had occurred many years previously. In disgrace with the Church of England following my abrupt departure from Ely Cathedral, I eventually went to stay briefly with Sydney Campbell who was now Organist of Canterbury Cathedral. Mildly he poured scorn on our record, *Music for the Feast of Christmas* causing me great pain – for my self-confidence was easily undermined. His own cathedral choristers fulfilled the description given by my Ely Head Boy of 1953; they sang like girls. Then in 1961 Boris Ord died. His last weeks and months he had spent in Gibbs buildings, confined to his rooms, cared for by a nurse, and playing endless games of Patience. It was a merciful release but, sadly, I could not but recall his enthusiasm, vigour and kindness to me when (but a few years before) we had driven to and from Cambridge in 'that yellow wagon'. But I did not attend his funeral in King's Chapel. A rotten cowardice kept me away from having to meet so many of my former colleagues and peers.

Next a Catholic friend from the Oratory suggested that I undertook the post of Director of Music to the Oblates of St Charles Borromeo at their church in Bayswater, an establishment which had been founded by Henry Manning in the days before he became Cardinal Archbishop of Westminster. Here I had in my charge a choir of ten professional singers and a beautiful old William Hill organ upon which to play. The principal Sunday service was, of course, the old Tridentine High Mass, and our repertoire (while always being scrupulously correct liturgically) was eclectic in every decent sense.

But there was a hidden snag. The Second Vatican Council was in full labour (Rome always moves slowly). Alas, when the cork was eventually pulled from the champagne bottle, no one was able to get it back again! One day, after some three and a half years of apparent security on the Rock of Peter, I was sent for by the Procurator who proceeded to put myself and my choral establishment under one month's notice. The then Superior of the Order vanished and was duly reported to have seceded from the priesthood. Latin was enthusiastically dropped; a deplorable vernacular welcomed in its place. Mass was to be celebrated facing West – as it were *at* the congregation – instead of East, as an offering and sacrifice on their behalf. High Altars became superfluous, the treasures of Gregorian chant and Renaissance polyphony but useless adjuncts, the music of the Roman Rite silenced. It was the hollow silence of death raped by proletarian babble.

To set against this negation was the fact that the Benedictine Order had always been associated with education and culture. There were the great schools like those of Ampleforth, Ealing and Downside. There was Ramsgate with its superb Pugin buildings. Ely, in common with many other cathedrals and great churches, had been a Benedictine House until the time of the Reformation. Thus, the collegiate choir of men and boys dated back in unbroken tradition for at least nine hundred years. And I had seen for myself the monks of Farnborough making the very best use of the revisions now imposed by Vatican II. With my experience and success in voicing and training cathedral choristers, I could only add lustre to all this. Finally there was the lure of the Cavaillé-Coll organ.

England generally speaking was still in a very bad way in terms of the organ considered as a musical instrument. The city of London had a few ancient chamber organs, lovingly preserved by Noel Mander. I would soon see that his firm should have care of the Cavaillé-Coll, for this was their *metier*. There was also the uncompromising work directed by Ralph Downes which had commenced amidst howls of fury with the grand instrument in the Royal Festival Hall. Niggle as the critics may, there is nothing wrong with this organ. It is simply that, acoustically speaking, it is in the wrong building – as are all orchestras, choirs, or what you will that perform there. The experts consulted certainly got their sums right by pencil and paper. In fact the end product just doesn't work and we still have to admit that sound is a great mystery. Should anyone require further convincing, one needs only to go and hear the organs in Brompton Oratory, Croydon Fairfield Hall, St Alban's and Gloucester Cathedrals; and they all stemmed from Downes having been sonically bowled over by the great Parisian masterpieces of Cavaillé-Coll. Alas, England being what it is, even today there is still plenty of Midland Mud being preserved and produced. Hence the age-old saw: 'there are musicians and there are organists'. I certainly wanted to be living in close proximity to this country's only Cavaillé-Coll.

Eventually a letter arrived from the Prior inviting me to become Organist at Farnborough and I duly accepted. But with Father O'Gorman's words about the 'Monkey Men' still in mind, I decided against relinquishing the tenancy of my home in St Leonards. In any case I would need somewhere to live during my post-Christmas and post-Easter breaks and during my summer holiday. Also I was anxious that Dushkin should always remain in the care of Justin Pryke. Some people might dismiss all this as mere sixth sense. I prefer the term 'Holy Ghost'.

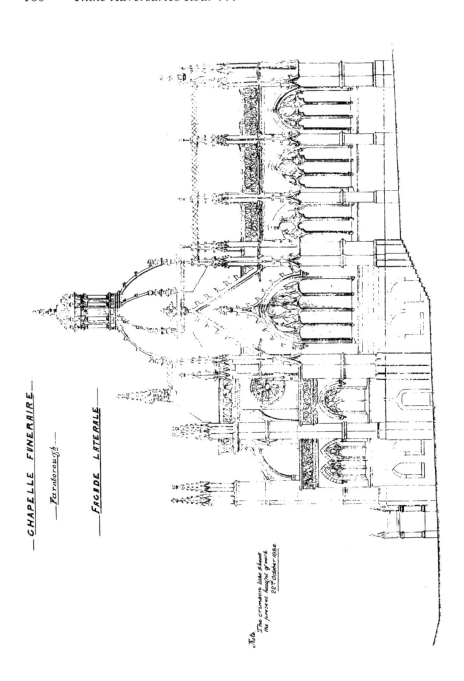

Chapter XI

St Michael's Abbey

September arriving, Dushkin and I set out on our journey to St Michael's Abbey. We drove through beautiful parts of Sussex, veering northwards after Horsham, and continued on where the environs became suspiciously 'stock-broker belt' Surrey; and so along the Hog's Back to Farnham. At this point an open main road turned us northwards amid the highly organised surrounds of Aldershot, and so to the far extremes of Farnborough itself where we once more turned to the west. Farnborough town appeared to consist mainly of multiple-storey car parks and quite hideous all-under-one-roof shopping emporia. Our road itself was obviously a very busy trunk connection leading to the motorways running to the north and west of England. Just before Farnborough Station we had to negotiate, in the face of oncoming traffic, a sharp right turn to the great Gates leading to the Abbey grounds.

A driveway took us up a steep hill bordered by dense woodland on the left, foliage concealed suburbia on the right. At the top a bend led us down behind all the forestry and so to the Abbey itself. We disembarked into welcome silence and approached the great Abbey door. I hauled on a substantial bell-pull and we proceeded to wait. The time was about four o'clock. Soon an elderly monk appeared, dumping our luggage in the cool ante-chamber, and said that the community were taking tea in the clearing at the rear and that we should go to join them. Negotiating another great door I found that we were now within the Enclosure proper (community members and their approved male guests only). We followed the monk along the main cloister to beneath the central bell tower with its ever ascending staircase around the walls. Being assured that Dushkin was not thirsty, he opened a small doorway and we emerged to find the household drinking tea and eating home-made cake and biscuits.

It was at this moment that Dushkin spotted the Prior's Burmese cat, and with a great shout of joy she streaked after it. Within seconds the cat was safely up a tree, leaving Dushkin to look first up the tree and then all around it and then, with a virtual shrug of the shoulders, to return saying that after all she had done her best. I was overcome with acute embarrassment, only to discover that the entire community including the Prior himself were convulsed with laughter. I was handed a mug of tea, asked to sit down, and to help myself to cake and biscuits as I chose. Thus I was made to feel more than welcome, as was Dushkin who could always get away with absolute murder!

Tea concluded, the Prior conducted me to my room. We ascended the great central staircase to the first level and then turned through a door into what was technically known as the Guest Wing, though still within the Enclosure. He opened a door to disclose a beautifully furnished bedroom and study combined, with a window looking out onto the south transept of the abbey church itself. Thick curtains hung from a wooden rod, there was an antique writing desk, two upright chairs, a book case awaiting my books, a small armchair and bedside table, reading lamp, bed, wash basin and wardrobe. Walls were negative grey-white, their only contents a crucifix, their only interruption an adjustable electric heating apparatus. Pale fawn carpet was fitted throughout; the door was of stripped oak. There was a telephone for my use in the passage outside.

Seating himself on one of the chairs, the Prior told me how, some twenty years previously when he was the Precentor, he had set up and trained the choir of boys and men, but that on being elected Prior he had had to relinquish this duty. Nevertheless, it was clear to me that not only was he strongly inclined musically, but that also all forms of art and architecture mattered to him fundamentally. He remarked on the restrained beauty of my plainsong accompaniments as he had heard them in the summer. I told him that they were all as I had absorbed that art from Ralph Downes.

Indeed, my indebtedness to Ralph Downes was incalculable as were the strict instructions in the arts of cerebral improvisation to the discussions and observations which I had received from Marcel Dupré. Also the strict routine of life as I now had to lead it suited me in every way as one who was travelling the road of a recovering alcoholic. Rising at 6.30 each morning, I would perform my ablutions, take Dushkin for a brief run in the grounds, and be ready on the organ bench at 8.00 a.m. for the commencement of the capitular Mass. Then to breakfast (informal with talking permitted, the arrival of the morning post, dealing with one's own washing up), after which a good walk with Dushkin and back to the church for a solid morning of practice. Dushkin was permitted to be with me during these work sessions, when she lay quietly beside me on the cool wood flooring.

The midday Office terminated my practice and at 12.20 or so, Dushkin having returned to my room, came the main meal of the day; standing until grace had been said, eating in silence while one of the monks read from a suitable book and two others waited on us; the general and talkative washing of dishes in the kitchen, and then, from 2.00 p.m. to 3.00 p.m., silence and rest. I soon found that I too needed this rest.

After this the monks returned to their various forms of employment, the Prior lovingly tending his apiary, and I was free until Vespers at 5.00 p.m. If it was a Saint's Day I would play a full *Sortie* at the conclusion of the service. We would have had tea, informally, in the late afternoon and our supper followed in the refectory at about 6.00 p.m. More practice until the community assembled for Compline and at 9.00 p.m. the Great Silence followed. Should one feel hungry during the later hours, one was permitted to raid the kitchen. Having been out behind the house with Dushkin, I would settle to preparing in my mind the music for Mass on the next day. The Proper, being set out in the Gradualia for the whole year, presented no problems, but I had the greatest difficulty in getting the Precentor to let me know in advance which of the plainchant Ordinarys (there are eighteen altogether) he proposed to use. This was a matter of great importance to me in predetermining various pitch relations involved. Yet all he had to do was to tell me before he retired for the night instead of rushing to the organ bench in those last few seconds before Mass commenced. Then one morning he was the Celebrant and he failed to appear . . . to be found still asleep in his bed! I was not privy to the upshot.

Gradually I assembled some of my more important books and pictures and, with Dushkin, my room began to feel truly like a second home. I usually confined my reading to the afternoon, my last chore of the day being to make myself thoroughly theoretically familiar with the music required for the next morning. Then, comfortable and easy sleep. The simple monastic side of things soon became a happy way of life. But not so matters concerning the Sunday choir of men and boys and their attendant rehearsals.

It seemed to have been assumed that, because of the reputation of my Ely choristers, I would be able to teach the Abbey boys the techniques of singing and then, seated at the piano, leave the Precentor to do the rest, choose and rehearse the music, conduct at Mass, and generally take to himself authority. It was not only that I myself was in no way given to tuning instruments for others to play, but the proposition was in any case totally impossible. No sooner had I finished my training sessions with the boys and handed them over than they lapsed back into their former ways as though I had never been. In fact, apart from my personal clothing of the Sunday Mass as an organist, things were rapidly going from very bad to much worse. Thoroughly depressed, I went to discuss the matter with the Prior.

With hindsight, I would have expected him to call a meeting of the three of us in order to try and thresh things out. He did nothing of the sort. Instead he demoted the Precentor from his rank and created me *Rector Chori*. So I made my first enemy. Several of the older boys left but in any case their voices would have been beyond redemption. Then the rumours started.

No one changed his behaviour towards me, but gradually and insidiously I was made aware that the choirmen were thoroughly fed up with me. I decided the only thing to do was to face them. On a Friday in that latter part of rehearsal which was reserved for work with them alone, I asked them to put down their music and to draw up their chairs and sit down. Taking a chair for myself I also sat down, facing them, and told them of all that had come to my ears, adding that if such was the case then I was perfectly prepared to resign. Seldom have I seen such blank astonishment and consternation. One of them (a lawyer by profession) told me that what I was supposing was absolute rubbish, that they all understood my difficulties, and that they all looked forward in due course to becoming a really fine choir under my training.

Of course my relief was enormous and, rather as I had done with the lay clerks at Ely, I told them of the immense difficulties with which we were faced, especially with regard to the recruitment of boys, and how it could only be a hard slog and a slow process. We parted that evening in an entirely new atmosphere and I was left to realise, without much difficulty, from whom the dagger of destruction was coming. Christmas was drawing near, I had the whole thing on my shoulders and, perforce, musically it wasn't very good. After playing for the Capitular Mass on Christmas Day, Dushkin and I returned to St Leonards.

To be at home again and by the sea was incredible. So, for Dushkin, was the great snow storm – a dog's idea of heaven. Cards of greeting without number awaited me, including one from Father O'Gorman. Old friends who had seen me through my final terrible days of conflict with alcohol made contact. I had long telephone conversations with Ralph Downes and George Malcolm. Whatever the future musical problems of the Abbey might be, it was not for me to be working the miracles. That curious sense of *déjà vu* was alive in me again. With all the stamina of a youthful sixty-two years of age I was soon thoroughly fit and healthy. And when, mid-January, after a splendid break, we returned to the Abbey, the miracles began to happen.

At first it was back to the same old impossible grind but with a seriously decimated number of choristers. The choir being situated in the north transept and the *Grand Orgue* standing behind the High Altar, we had to resort more and more to unaccompanied Mass settings and motets. Obviously, I could not be in two places at once and closed circuit television was of no help. Then, by some means which I now forget, I made contact with the Headmistress of the local Catholic Primary School. She said that she would submit to me for audition a selection of the brighter boys aged between eight and nine years. Those that I chose could attend probationary rehearsals with me in the school during the final period on Wednesday afternoons as well as attending all practices and Sunday Solemn Mass at the Abbey. In this way I found some half a dozen eminently suitable voices to work on and began intensive training in the manner which had been so successful with my beloved choristers at Ely. The effect on general morale with both the existing Abbey choristers and with the choirmen was immediate, and things soon began to give signs of moving in the right direction. Of course nothing became established, as it were, 'over night', nor did I expect it to do so. For several weeks it was the inevitable quasi-Sisyphus situation. I would seem nearly to have got the boulder to the top of the hill when it would promptly proceed once again to crash down to the bottom. Nevertheless, by Easter the whole choir was becoming integrated, and I instituted a short pre-Solemn Mass rehearsal on Sunday mornings so that they never had to go into singing the service 'cold'. It was all so absorbing and exciting that I was unaware of any particular strain or stress upon myself. Then one Sunday, having concluded playing the *sortie*, I turned from the organ to find a young man waiting for me.

He introduced himself as Anthony Noble and presented me to his wife Sarah. As a graduate of Trinity College, London, he was an organist and harpsichordist and had recently come to Farnborough as Director of Music at the Silesian College. Did I require any assistance at the Abbey? I told him that my need for help with the musical performances was desperate, but that I had been told by the Prior that there was no money available to pay for this. Anthony said that as far as he was concerned this did not matter. He would be only too glad to observe my methods and to play accompaniments and, if it could be made available, have time when he might practise on the Cavaillé-Coll organ; then he would be more than satisfied. I introduced him to the Prior and it was agreed that we might proceed in this manner, Anthony being like myself supplied with a necessary set of keys. And so came about the second of two miracles in the space of one term, with Anthony being acknowledged on the music lists formally as 'Sub-organist'.

Without any prompting from me, Anthony made it his business to attend every single choir practice and choral service and, between us, we now embarked on the makings of a really challenging repertoire. Also his playing was positively virtuoso and we more or less shared the performing of the post-Mass *Sorties*. At last choir music by Mozart, Haydn, Schubert and Fauré ceased to be a mere pipe-dream. The boys were developing a fine resilient tone, and control of diction and tuning improved all round. Moreover Anthony and Sarah were quick to see that total life 'within the walls' was taxing me, and Dushkin and I spent many happy evenings with them at their home. They also gave me a set of keys so that I could take refuge at any time during the day.

However, with our reassembly after the Easter break, I began to notice two things. One was the marked appreciation shown by members of the congregation for the music at the *Missa Cantata*, many of them remaining in their seats until the final chords of the organ *sortie*; the other was that, apart from the Celebrant, fewer and fewer of the Abbey community were bothering to attend – obviously considering that their earlier attendance at a Low Mass fulfilled their duty for the day. There seemed to be coming about an implied split between them and the cultural gifts which the Abbey had to offer. This did not perturb me particularly to begin with, but it was something which was to lead to dire consequences in the future. The summer term swept along with ever increasing style and panache until, towards its end, a new stress and strain was imposed on us.

Some considerable time previously, the Prior had arranged that with the arrival of August the choir would go into residence for a week in order to sing the daily Evensong and Sunday Eucharist at Norwich Cathedral. This meant not only learning to chant Anglican chants to the Prayer Book psalter but also making up a repertoire of Canticle settings – all of them things totally foreign to the choir of St Michael's Abbey. I used the Preces by Thomas Hunt as I had edited them for Woburn Square and Ely. The Psalms I pointed myself, relying on my memory of the Ely psalter and for the chants I thought it best to make a selection for men's voices only. Latin would present no problem for the Sunday Eucharist and would be acceptable for weekday anthems. For settings of the Magnificat and Nunc Dimittis we managed Stanford in C, Wesley in F, and the 'Dorian' service by Tallis. There would have to be some repetition. The Sunday Eucharist was Schubert in G, a plainsong Credo, and Mozart's *Ave verum corpus*. The Dean of Norwich was the dignified celebrant, using the text of the Book of Common Prayer.

The choristers were housed near the Cathedral close, in the care of one of the monks who was a comparative stranger to me. He was assisted by two of the parents, acting as lady-matrons. I, with Anthony and Sarah and the men of the choir, were a little way from the city centre in a lodging where we each had our own small room and communal bathing and shower facilities. Each morning I would drive in to the choristers' house and, following breakfast, take their main rehearsal of the day. Then I would proceed to a neighbouring building and go through the same programme with the men. After that it was freedom until the pre-Evensong full practice in the Cathedral song-room. The Dean asked me to go to see him and I was relieved and delighted to find that he had been a King's, Cambridge, choral scholar under Boris Ord and that he not only shared my enthusiasm for the old Great Western Railway but also had a number of beautifully engineered fine-scale models in his study. We talked about Patrick Hankey and the days at Ely.

But I was most disturbed to discover that during the day the choristers were either being left to run wild or were playing games of leap frog and catch-as-catch-can with the monk. They could not be expected to give of their best as singers in these circumstances. At Ely, my choristers were only allowed to go swimming or for long-distance runs on 'plain' days since such exertions upset their singing control both physically and sonically. And in Norwich there was so much of historical and cultural interest for the Farnborough boys to be shown. Furthermore their first duty as choristers was to the cathedral. That was why we were there. The monk disagreed with me. We were there for a holiday and the cathedral was secondary. If I was not prepared to change my attitude, he would telephone the Prior and have me called back to the Abbey. Anthony Noble said if I went, he would go too. Naturally, this was all very tense. The monk did telephone but was told to leave things as they were. There would be a discussion upon our return in the following week.

The Abbey choir managed to acquit itself creditably at all services and particularly so at the Sunday Eucharist, Anthony and myself receiving the Dean's warmest thanks. At Farnborough the monk with whom I had had my disagreement was not in evidence but Dushkin *was* (very much so) leaving no one in doubt of her joy in having me with her again. So back to St Leonards and the sea, back to home and old friends, to freedom and leisure and the beautiful inland country of Sussex. For three weeks it was pure holiday, but then came the return to St Michael's Abbey.

It was of course a joy to be back again with my choristers and choirmen and to be getting under way with the autumn programme of music; also to be playing and practising once more on the glorious Cavaillé-Coll organ. Nothing was said to me about the incidents at Norwich. But I was nearer the edge than I was aware. Day by day we worked our way through the month with its culmination in my name day: the Feast of St Michael and All Angels. What a glorious Solemn Mass that was with its Proper plainsong, its Haydn and Victoria, and sharp in my memory my playing of the *Finale* from Widor's Sixth Symphony. Then something snapped.

Avoiding everybody I went straight to my room and sat down. Sounds of festivity came up from below and sounds of the Community preparing for a truly festive meal with wines, to be followed by coffee and liqueurs in their own special withdrawing room. I sat and stared blankly with Dushkin at my feet. Time passed. I felt totally detached. Eventually, in the afternoon, there was a knock at my door.

It was Dom Robert who had so kindly cared for Dushkin during my absence in Norwich. He said my non-appearance at the feast had been noticed. Was I alright? I said that I wasn't, but I could not explain why. Infuriatingly I was very nearly in tears. I asked him please to tell the Prior that I was packing a few belongings and with Dushkin would be returning to St Leonards that afternoon. I would be seeing my doctor on the next day. Poor Robert. He was a good and caring man and I had left him to carry the can.

Back at home I slept heavily and duly went to the surgery on the Monday morning. It seemed to me difficult to know what to say to a busy doctor with a crowd of people waiting to see him. There suddenly seemed to be nothing specific. And then I started weeping. With great patience he gradually heard the whole story and told me that I was in a state of emotional collapse and confusion. He would give me some sedation and I was to stay quietly at home. In two days time *he* would call on *me*. We could then consider what it might be best to do.

When on Wednesday the doctor did call I was certainly in a much more stable frame of mind. His suggestion was that if I were to return to the Abbey now I might well end up in a far more serious state than I had already reached and that, as a recovering alcoholic, I would certainly be foolhardy in taking any such risk. With my permission he would write to the Prior saying that it was his considered opinion that I ought not to return to Farnborough before Christmas and that, at this stage, he was not able to say whether or not I ought to return at all. To this I agreed, only too glad to have the load taken off my shoulders.

After a few weeks I received a rather cold letter from the Prior. If it was not my intention to return, would I please have my room cleared of all my personal effects. In other words, the sack! A good friend with a very large estate car came over and listed with me every possible item that should come back to my St Leonards home and he duly drove over to the Abbey and retrieved the lot. Then, thank God, things began almost to assume an air of comedy.

Anthony Noble telephoned to ask if he and Sarah might come to see me and we arranged that they should stay overnight. He said that the Prior had been begging him to take on the post of *Rector Chori* at an increased stipend merely to deal with training the choir and conducting them at the Sunday Mass. Money would be found to pay for an assistant organist. He had told the Prior that he could agree to nothing without first of all consulting me. Meanwhile the choristers and choir-men all sent me their best wishes.

My response was that there was nothing that I could wish for more than that he should now take over the position of *Rector Chori*, but that I in my turn would ask for certain conditions to be attached. It had long been my wish to make CD recordings of the works of César Franck, the instrument differing but little from that in what had been Franck's own church, that of *Sainte-Clotilde* in Paris. If he could persuade the Prior to agree to this, then I could think of nothing better than that he should succeed me at the Abbey. To this Anthony readily agreed, and a tribute to his own success was eventually to be shown in their splendid record-ing of the Fauré *Requiem* with the organ part played by Simon Williamson and the baritone solos sung by Sean Clarke. (Herald HAVPC 117).

So my own future with Cavaillé-Coll became assured and I was also invited to give a public recital in the Abbey church, when I played Bach (including the celebrated Toccata and Fugue in D minor) and French music culminating in Guilamnt's notorious *Grand Choeur* in D major. The applause was tumultuous. The fee, £10!

PARISH OF OUR LADY & SAINT MICHAEL, FARNBOROUGH

(Affiliated to the Royal School of Church Music)
Order of Music at the Abbey Church of Saint Michael
For full details of services please see church notice boards, or telephone Farnborough 546105

Dom David Higham, OSB (Prior, Parish Priest)
Michael Howard, Hon. ARAM (Rector Chori)
Anthony Noble, GTCL (hons.) *(Sub-organist)*

SEPTEMBER 1985

Sunday 8 XXIII of the year	1015	SOLEMN MASS:	Missa de Ecclesia Christi – *Howard;* Plainsong G
		Introit:	Iustus es Domine
		Gradual:	Beata gens
		Alleluia:	Domine exaudi orationem
		Hymns:	446 (L 375 omit v.3); 424
		Motet:	Ave verum corpus – *Elgar*
		Voluntary:	Les Enfants de Dieu – *Olivier Messiaen*

Sunday 15 XXIV of the year	1015	SOLEMN MASS:	Mass in G major – *Schubert;* Plainsong F
		Introit:	Da pacem Domine
		Gradual:	Lætatus sum
		Alleluia:	Timebunt gentes
		Hymns:	147, 562
		Motet:	Crux fidelis – *Ioannes Rex*
		Voluntary:	Prelude & Fugue in B minor S.544 – *J.S. Bach*
	1830	SOLEMN VESPERS & Benediction	
		Antiphon:	Whoever loses his life
		Magnificat:	*Tallis in the Dorian mode*
		Motet:	Ave verum corpus K.618 – *Mozart*
		Voluntary:	Toccata – *Eugene Gigout*

Sunday 22 XXV of the year	1015	SOLEMN MASS:	*Plainsong C*
		Introit:	Salus populi ego sum
		Gradual:	Dirigatur oratio mea
		Alleluia:	Confitemini Domino
		Hymns:	442, 329
		Motet:	Cantate Domino
		Voluntary:	Prelude & Fugue in G minor – *Dietrich Buxtehüde*

Sunday 29 SAINT MICHAEL	1015	SOLEMN MASS:	Missa Sancte Ioannes de Deo – *Haydn;* Plainsong H
		Introit:	Benedicite Dominum
		Gradual:	Benedicite Dominum
		Alleluia:	Sancte Michael Archangeli
		Hymns:	242, 395
		Motet:	O quam gloriosum est – *Victoria*
		Voluntary:	Finale (Symphonie VI) – *Charles-Marie Widor*

Chapter XII

Storm and Stress

In the days before my appointment to St Michael's Abbey, a particular friend of mine had been the Reverend David Jarmy who was the senior curate of Christ Church, St Leonards. He was extremely musical and had a fine tenor voice. Originally it had been his intention to become a professional singer and he had studied with that great artist Ian Partridge. On finding that his true vocation lay with the priesthood he nevertheless still fulfilled in the Sussex area various engagements, undertaking the Evangelist in Bach's St Matthew and St John Passions and the tenor arias in Handel's Messiah. There was a fine grand piano at the west end of Christ Church where I used to accompany him and, at his invitation, coach him in such matters as diction and dramatic presentation.

David was also something of a gourmand and an enterprising cook. Not infrequently I would take superb luncheons with him in his spacious and well-furnished room in the clergy house; no mere examples of cooking, these meals, but cooking elevated to a fine art. Dushkin was always welcome at these feasts, as she was in the church when we were rehearsing. But when we returned from Hampshire, David had gone.

Christ Church was of absolute Anglo-Catholic persuasion and even went so far as to use the English translation from the Roman Missal at Mass. Its tradition was that of the SECR which some people mistook for South East and Chatham Railway but in reality surely must stand for 'South East Coast Religion'! So naturally all clergy at Christ Church must be celibates. I knew that David had for some time been wrestling with his situation at Christ Church and the fact that he had become enamoured of a young nurse named Elizabeth. He had decided that marriage was the correct answer and, having notified the Bishop, had accepted the living of Sidley a few miles inland from Bexhill. Learning that I was back in circulation I was invited with Dushkin to go and spend Christmas.

Thus followed for me a truly enjoyable and relaxed 'Noel' happily divorced from all the *stürm und drang* of the previous few months. The guest room of the vicarage was twin-bedded, one occupied by myself and the other by Dushkin who had brought her own bedding. The house was spacious with a fully fitted kitchen and laundry section attached; the main living room comfortable and warm with open fireplace, stereo, radio, and David's vast collection of records. His own study was immediately inside the front door and contained his library. The church itself was spacious and good acoustically, if not very distinguished. The organ, indifferent, but available to me then and throughout the future as I might wish for my own practice. To the rear was a huge field completely fenced, in which Dushkin could frolic at will. I discovered that Elizabeth's uncle 'Vic' was the Victor who used to drive over from Hastings before the war to play the organ in Winchelsea Parish Church.

It was nice to be back in my own home and to invite friends to meals and to stay. It was nice to be visiting the local shops and to discover a real general store and delicatessen where Dushkin too was also welcome and made much of. It was nice to drive and walk with her along the banks of the great Military Canal in all kinds of weather. It was nice regularly to visit Sidley to see the Jarmys and to begin serious technical preparation of the César Franck works which I hoped in due course to be commercially recording on the Cavaillé-Coll at St Michael's Abbey. It was a compliment that David and Elizabeth asked me to go and live in the Sidley Vicarage while they were away on holiday. Once more I was thoroughly fit and healthy and full of zest. Then came the hurricane.

It was in the early hours of night that I was awakened by a tremendous mighty rushing wind. Worrying about Dushkin I went into the sitting room to find her, huddled and distraught, upon the sofa. The wind increased in its noise and fury and, putting my arms about her and leaning over her, I held her gently and talked to her. Outside as the rage increased it seemed as if the whole building was beginning to rock. Then came the first ripping noise of slates torn from the roof, followed by the shattering crash as they splintered on the ground below. On and on it went, seeming ever to gain in merciless power. By dawn there was some abatement and with the beginnings of daylight I could see trees simply ripped up and flung about as it were by some spoilt child; the road a mass of rubble; cars overturned; two enormous trunks lying athwart my own vehicle which was, astoundingly, undamaged. Water and electricity had failed and many houses had their windows blown in. In the distance one could hear the surge and roar of the sea as it smashed its way into the promenade. The telephone was dead.

When things began to quieten I got dressed and we went outside. Somebody had found a stand-pipe and was filling buckets of water.

People, normally complete strangers, were talking to each other in a way that I had not seen since the high days of the Blitz. Everyone wanted to help somebody else. Some were distressed about their animals; others about their false teeth. A man who had a calor gas stove came out with thermos flasks of sweet black coffee. The English with their backs against the wall . . . all inhibitions gone.

Later David Jarmy appeared. Somehow, by some freak, he and Elizabeth had not been hit quite so directly. Together we moved all my belongings into my front room. At the rear of the house there were sinister cracks through which one could see daylight. We managed partially to drag away the branches of a tree that was blocking my car. Then he insisted that I pack a suitcase and move over to be with them at Sidley. It is as well that we did not remain in St Leonards. The next day came the rain and with it the falling of both my rear ceilings, bringing with them that disgusting over-sweet sour smell that goes with sodden plaster.

It now came to light that the property in which I had my maisonette had been put into the hands of an estate agent. Of course he wanted me out but, since I was a sitting tenant, there was nothing he could do about it. So he tried offering me £2000 to make myself scarce. David advised me to make no response to this and he put me in touch with his own solicitors. Then came what is known in the 'film rights' world as the bumping up process. Eventually I settled for £5000 and costs and put all my belongings into storage. So Dushkin and I continued for the time being to live with the Jarmys. How they stood it I just don't know, but never at any time was there the slightest indication that they did not actually enjoy having us on their premises. *Sicut regnum* . . .

I now started casting around for somewhere to play as organist, once again combing the advertisements in the *Church Times*. Few locations were within reach, but one at Groombridge seemed possible. I wrote and was asked by the vicar, Father Michael Henley, to go to see him. In appearance Father Henley was very much the traditional Anglican High Church priest; black suit, black stock, narrow clerical collar, a gentle manner. He had been trained at Chichester theological college. He took me into his library, a room literally walled with books, and we began to talk. He explained that Groombridge proper was some half a mile away eastwards and in Kent. We were in New Groombridge which had been built as a railway town serving the line from Tunbridge Wells West which duly split north for Victoria or London Bridge and south for Lewes and various towns on the coast. Now it was all closed and Groombridge Station derelict. St Thomas' Church had been built in the 1880s to designs by Norman Shaw who, during the 1860s, had built two country houses in the neighbourhood, Glen Andred and Leyswood. St

Thomas' was of course a church of the 'SECR' tradition, but now all was changed as was the ever growing population of the town.

I began to ask Father Michael specific questions and I suspect that he did not really like what he had to tell me. The Hymnal was the New English Hymnal and the two Mass settings in use were both by composers not generally known and used the Series A texts. Hymns were supplemented by the more 'pop' inclined collection, *Mission Praise*. Choir voices were some sopranos, no alto, one tenor, two basses, the organ an old Grey and Davison 'house' organ in a beautiful case.

The Churchwardens, Trevor Wells and Mrs Rosamund Steel, would be joining us shortly so that they could ask and answer any questions that might arise. Choir practice was on Thursday evenings for one hour; the Sunday service was the Parish Eucharist. I asked him did he use the Prayer Book for the 8.00 a.m. celebration but gathered that it would not have been welcomed.

I might as well say at once that Michael Henley was a scholar and a gentleman. During his meals, taken alone, he listened to classical music. He went each day into the church and knelt unobtrusively to recite his daily Office. He spent his entire time visiting the elderly, the sick, the hospitals and the nursing homes in the area. He was delightful company with an unexpected sense of fun. He possessed a selflessness and a certain serenity without any thought of return. When he retired it was the total end of an era as far as Groombridge was concerned.

Mrs Steel asked me a number of questions, but I cannot recall what they were. A stipend was offered which was acceptable and wedding and funeral fees for organ music were also agreed. Trevor Wells asked me to go over to the church with him and inspect the organ. He took at once to Dushkin who had been waiting in my car and she now joined us. I played various Bach pieces which worked quite well. Straight pedal board (good) but concave (bad); also narrow scale. The keyboard to pedal board distance relations were wrong, suggesting some interference with the manuals. But, all in all, interesting, and it reminded me of the far far larger Grey and Davison that had stood at the west end of St Pancras Church in London before the war. At Groombridge the second keyboard stopped at tenor C but a double flute made certain transpositions and combinations possible. In both musical and mechanical terms it fascinated Trevor Wells – a fact that was to land us both in future trouble.

But first the choir. Attendance at practice did not ensure attendance on Sunday. Attendance on Sunday was not governed by attendance on Thursday. My attempt to correct this was respected by most of them, but some chose to go their own way and openly to defy me, putting morale at risk and my authority in danger of ridicule. Thus, manners apart, the lute was at once riven. And second the use of the organ. I would play a suitable prelude before the Eucharist began – Bach, Couperin, de Grigny. The assembling congregation would chatter away happily. Greeting of friends? Social gossip? Character assassination? I wouldn't know. But at the end it was a case of play out the choir and stop, for the place at once became a vociferous crowd of coffee drinkers and that was that. Dispirited, I would leave by a door behind the organ. On one occasion I passed two men standing. One was saying: 'What the poor old Church of England is coming to, I just don't know.'

However, there was the organ and the fact that it was upon this instrument that I would now be maintaining my abilities as an executant; and in this sphere I had the enthusiastic interest of Trevor Wells, this man of such unexpectedly diversified talents and abilities. No one seemed at all clear as to where the instrument had come from and the firm of Grey and Davison had long been defunct. It was now 'tuned' twice a year by a representative from Hill, Norman and Beard. I demonstrated to Trevor that while, overall, its gentle tones were pleasing, there were three things that could be done to give it far more lyrical body and plangency. Each manual chorus was topped by a two-foot rank. (That is to say, if you drew this stop and played middle C, the pitch you got was the C two octaves above). These ranks contributed nothing other than a toppy whistling. The answer would be to transpose the pipes so that the Great two-foot became a Quint, giving centre to the chorus, and the Swell two-foot became a Tierce, providing bite and singing sharpness to the sound. Likewise, the Trumpet rank on the Great (the only reed stop on the instrument) was thin at the top, too rounded in the middle, and ineffective in the bass ..., all this showing that there were weights on the tongues and that the wind pressure was wrong. So we got down to it, I sitting at the keyboards, Trevor performing wonders of contortion to cope with the work from inside the case itself. At last it was complete after many arduous sessions and the pipes that had become spare were stored on top of the case itself. It was a revelation, not just for the music of Bach and his contemporaries – but also Guilmant, Widor, Franck and Vierne could now be played with some style and authenticity. In celebration I gave a public recital of Franck's *Trois Chorals*. Our changing of the block regulators to the three composition pedals did much to facilitate this.

There is one thing which I can say without equivocation on behalf of the human race; life would be sadly lacking in entertainment without it. Not troubling their manners to mention it to me and waiting until a time when Trevor Wells was away, the Parochial Church Council ordered Hill, Norman and Beard to return the organ specification to what it had been before. Not that that achieved anything of worth, for no one knew what the original specifications of the organ or organs had been and the records of Grey and Davison had long since been destroyed. But it was a good ploy on behalf of mediocrity and that's what the public likes best!

Meanwhile I was homeless and so made application to the Wealden District Council. Dushkin and I were given temporary shelter by yet another staunch friend who lived in the country immediately outside Wadhurst. Again, whatever the stress and strain this arrangement caused to her, we were never made to feel anything other than thoroughly welcome. The house was bursting with books; the fields around ideal for walks; and the distance from Groombridge no more than seven or eight miles. And then I was offered a two-roomed ground floor flat with spacious ground around it at the top end of Groombridge, at the point where the road turns off and goes away into open country. Installing my books and the necessary furnishings that this small space would accommodate, I gave the balance of my belongings to that great friend who had seen me through my catastrophic nightmare so many years previously in Ghent. She had just bought a beautiful upper maisonette in a Regency house in Broadstairs.

So we settled down. Above me lived an elderly lady, a Mrs Fry, to whom Dushkin took an instant liking. My next door neighbour was Ron, a former signalman at Eridge junction box in the days when railways had been railways. Close by was Gordon, one-time fireman and driver on the line from Tunbridge Wells West via Groombridge to Victoria and London Bridge. Both of these new friends were always happy to talk 'shop' with me, appreciating my own obsessions with the trains we had all once known and loved. As far as I was concerned I was obviously in a cleft stick with St Thomas' Church and so asked Father Henley to accept my resignation. Nevertheless he remained a true and caring friend to me until his retirement and removal to Lewes. And Trevor Wells asked me if I would take on his son Jeremy as an organ pupil.

Jeremy and I commenced absolutely from scratch. He remained in my care as an organ student for some five years and eventually took full music graduation from the University at Guildford. Perforce I continued to have access to the Church and a young girl from a school in Tunbridge Wells came to me as another student starting from the beginning. She had also excellent potential as a trumpeter and finally went to read music at Exeter University. Of course, this teaching imposed upon myself all the discipline required to communicate and explain in a lucid manner, thus keeping me ever fresh and recreative.

Then, on one of our routine visits to St Leonards, Justin Pryke told me that Dushkin had developed a tumour on her liver and that it was inoperable. I asked him how long she might have left but he could not say; it might be eight days, eight weeks, possibly more, but she would not suffer. I would know when the time had come and I was to telephone him then, at any time, and to bring her down to the surgery where he would meet us. Otherwise, apart from changing her diet to boiled rice and fresh boiled chicken, let her carry on just as she might wish. The mercy was that she didn't know.

In fact it was for another eight months that Dushkin lived a happy if slightly slower life. Then one day she refused food. The next day, obviously weaker, she refused water. It was Sunday 3rd March 1991. She sat in my hallway and looked at me clearly: 'I have cared for you for the past fifteen years. Please care for me now.' I telephoned Justin, carried her to my car and we set off on our last journey together. At the surgery she lay in my arms on the table while Justin administered to her. He then left the room. I put my head gently against hers and talked to her, my tears running freely into her fur. Everything was very still. After some fifteen minutes Justin returned and said 'Michael, you can leave her now. She has gone.' I made arrangements that she should be cremated, thanked Justin for all that he had done for her throughout her life, and drove home.

My flat seemed huge, bleak, cold and empty; the whole purpose knocked out of existence. Worn out I went to bed and when I awakened at dawn the next morning, all the birds were singing.

Chapter XIII

The Sorrows of Death

(Day 3 Evening Prayer)

I soon came to realise that this state of rancid self-pity was the most infamous tribute of all that I could be paying to Dushkin. In fact it was *no* tribute, but an insult motivated by all that was lowest in my nature. Not for this had she cared so assiduously all those years, rejoicing in my joys and knowing that she had all my love and protection simply as a matter of course. I had been an insane and alcoholic wreck when, at the age of eight weeks, she had come to live with me. Her first concern ever was to see me balanced, happy, and fulfilled. For this she had trained me. Were I now to go to bits I would simply be destroying her whole *raison d'être*. Furthermore, as my friends were quick to point out, her life's work could never die unless I myself chose to kill it. One has only to read the closing pages of Axel Munthe's *Story of San Michele* to learn that in the end, in spite of the fulminating judges and the pomposity of the Twelve Apostles, Saint Rocco is waiting to conduct the likes of me to his own heaven where he cares for all the canine species. Work, work, work, recreate, and be glad. Where was my faith, shivering rag though it may be?

In 1985 I had recorded as a *Tribute to Cavaillé-Coll* movements from various works by Olivier Messiaen and Louis Vierne, together with an improvisation by myself which I later noted down from dictation and had published. The recording was issued and I now felt that it was time to turn to CD recordings of César Franck's organ music. The first of these was completed in September 1989 and included the *Fantasies* of 1860 and 1878 and the Pastorale of 1862. The second was not completed until 1992 following a seventieth birthday recital which I had given in Ely Cathedral. This CD comprised the 1878 *Cantabile* and *Les Trois Chorals* of 1890. These latter, composed in the August and September, were Franck's last compositions. An ailing man following an accident with a horse-bus in Paris, he probably never heard them played on the organ of *Sainte-Clotilde*, dying in the November of that year. Ironically, I too was suffering from the effects of a slight stroke and my heart began to play ducks and drakes. Collapsing, I was whisked to Guy's Hospital to have a pacemaker inserted. Eventually, back in good health, I discovered that God was still intent on moving in a mysterious way ... a veritable Hound of Heaven!

It was 13th August 1994; dry, hard, a scorcher of a day. Sally, my friend from Wadhurst, was wishing to acquire a pair of donkeys (Jennies of course) to take up residence in a paddock which she had recently bought. So far she had had no luck and I offered to go to see if there might be anything suitable at a Sanctuary some few miles north of Groombridge. There was a donkey with its inseparable companion, a goat, but they were not on offer. But I had to pass by the dog pound, a great sweltering concrete area with literally no shade. Some six or seven dogs were fighting madly by the wire fence while away on the far side lay the miserable bundle of a tri-coloured rough coat Collie bitch. I went to the office and said that I proposed to take her away – what did they want for her?

Some of these institutions would appear to be run on rather macabre lines. The bitch was named Emma and had been brought in only on the previous day. She was a thoroughbred but they could give me no history. They were not entitled to charge any price for her, but if I wanted her I could make a donation to their funds. Asking one of the men to go and fetch her, I wrote out a cheque for £50. When Emma arrived she gave all the signs of being in a state of complete mental blank. Put on a leash she walked beside me – not in front, not behind – as far as my car while I talked to her gently all the way. Opening a rear door she willingly got in and I removed her leash but kept all the windows nearly closed. When we got home I took her leash and came to open the back door. But I had no sooner begun than she was gone – running frantically down a lane that led to the main road. I tore after her, only to see her race straight into the traffic. Running madly I too was soon in the midst of traffic when a kindly lorry driver pulled in to the side, left wide open his driving door, and himself blocked all oncoming vehicles. But Emma simply turned and raced back the way she had come, myself doing my failing best to keep her in sight.

I went home, telephoning the police and anyone else I could think of in the town. Many people saw her galloping like a vixen with the hounds on her tail; eventually she went into a cul-de-sac and an ever-dear friend following her got out of her car, leaving the doors open. Emma thought 'safety' and leaped in, and so was brought home to me ... so she lived over the weekend behind closed doors, only going out on the leash (never once did she fail to ask), and clearly in a state of first class nervous breakdown. She was terrified, she didn't know me or anyone else, she didn't know where she was or why. Yet never did she attempt to bite me. Poor wreck of a dog, it makes me sick to remember her state, and to this day one has no idea of what nightmare she had been through. For the first two nights I slept with her beside me on the floor and she accepted a little food. Then on the Tuesday I was able to telephone Justin Pryke and take her straight to see him. Passively she allowed him to make a thorough examination but her dew claws has grown in complete circles and repenetrated the pelt. It meant a full operation and then a dreary few weeks wearing gaiters. Justin treated her with the rest of her inoculations, weighed her, prescribed her diet and said that he would like to see her weekly for a while. Then, with the help of a calm life of love and proper grooming, she gradually became transformed. As I write this, it is her birthday *circa* nine years – and there is no more gorgeous rough coat Collie bitch in East Sussex! She will bully me if she gets the chance, but she knows who is boss. As to music: I have to listen to my gramophone records by means of headphones and the two Franck CDs have sold successfully (Herald HAVPCD 125 and 147). Emma has a fine singing voice – we don't need gramophone records!

But there was still one more surprise to round off my career as an active musician. In 1972 I had conducted *Cantores in Ecclesia* in two programmes for Basil Lam. Entitled 'Purcell at Westminster Abbey' they were pre-recorded in the Royal Festival Hall with Margaret Phillips playing the organ. Containing what must rank among the finest of his output in this idiom, the music gave unlimited scope to the abilities of Geoffrey Mitchell, Peter Hall and David Thomas as counter-tenor, tenor, and bass soloists. In 1995 all the music was remastered onto a single CD (BBCRD 9126) and issued on the public market. In the first year alone I collected royalties in excess of £80, and my wonderful singers and colleagues at least collected a more than well deserved metaphorical bouquet.

Yet, looking around one today, one might well be tempted to ask to what purpose all this labour? To what end these principles? Tradition, ritual, rubrics, style, manners that makyth man – turn what way one will, the stench of their burning and destruction has at last burst into a flame that cannot be ignored; for some would have us believed that the time has come when there shall be no more commitment.

Chapter XIV

Usurpation

After my disastrous and to me humiliating experience with the church in New Groombridge I began to cast around again, watching the *Church Times*. A vacancy occurred at Roffey, a somewhat *in limbo* suburban town lying between Horsham and Crawley. I telephoned Father Alan, the pleasantly spoken priest there, and after some exchange of mutual information it was agreed that I should drive over to see him. He said that coming on the road from Horsham I could not miss the church which stood back in a spacious field and that he would meet me there. The church itself was a pleasing and spacious building with a south-east tower, built by A.W. Blomfield who had been noted for his superb restoration of the nave of Southwark Cathedral. The Sunday morning service was an Anglo-Catholic Mass sung by the congregation either to Merbecke or the Folk Mass by Martin Shaw; the organ, mechanical action early Walker, quite pleasing in its own way. Hymns were from the authentic English Hymnal.

The nave, aisled only to the north, was furnished with decent rush chairs rather than pews and was light and airy. The acoustic was good. The narrow 'quire' housed the organ on the south side together with the bell tower. The Sanctuary was mean, made the more so by the moving a few feet west of the High Altar, for Mass was celebrated *at* the congregation. But there were the proper candles, incense was used and the correct vestments worn. There was no choir and the congregation were expected to pull their weight ably led by Father Alan who had an excellent singing voice. Accompaniment apart, the more I could clothe the Mass with Prelude, Postlude and interim Improvisations, the better. The stipend was reasonable and there would be a contribution to my travelling expenses. I liked all this very much and I was drawn to Father Alan. A musical man, he frequently attended concerts in London and also enjoyed cooking and keeping house for himself and his guests.

Alan was also a priest of authority. People behaved with decent reverence when in church until I began my post-Mass *Sortie*. I spoke to him about this and he said: 'Don't worry. Just leave it until I am giving out the Notices next Sunday.' And he read them the riot act on manners in no uncertain terms. The effect was both immediate and productive. Those that so wished concluded their prayers and went over to the neighbouring Hall for tea and biscuits. The remainder sat in silence until I had played the last chord of whatever the piece might be then, to my surprise and pleasure, burst into applause . . . often afterwards asking who was the composer and when had he lived. So I made many new friends.

The church was always well filled and a large proportion of these people had driven in from the country surrounding because they liked the liturgy, Father Alan's forthright homilies, and my playing. But it was a long drive each way for me and after a time I found that I just could not keep it up. However, before I left we arranged for Anthony Noble to come over and give a harpsichord recital in which he played a programme of French music from *Le Grand Siècle* with that *panache* which has become so very much his own. I have held no church appointment since those days.

It was now that I began to concentrate my attention upon what was and in many a case what was *not* going on in the name of the Church of England. In 1981 Dean Edward Carpenter had appointed Simon Preston to be Organist and Master of the Choristers at Westminster Abbey. Dr Carpenter was an absolute traditionalist. In other words, like Dean Patrick Hankey of Ely in the 1950s and 60s, everything was observed precisely according to the Book of Common Prayer and its uncompromising rubrics. Simon Preston had already experienced this *modus vivendi* first as Organ Scholar at King's College, Cambridge, then during the five years he had been assistant to Sir William McKie at the Abbey. He had continued in the same vein during the next twelve years as Organist of Christ Church, Oxford, and as a brilliant organist and choirmaster was ideally suited to succeed to the Abbey. But after three years Dr Carpenter retired, to be followed by a man of very different calibre and one who was very much more to the way of thinking of the vice-Dean and his colleagues. Things began to change radically and in ways that directly affected the traditional choral repertoire.

The Abbey had boasted among its previous organist such great names as Orlando Gibbons, John Blow, Henry Purcell; and there was, from 1819 until 1831, that wonderful trainer of the singing voice Thomas Greatorex who had himself studied with Santarelli in Rome and Ignaz Pleyel in Strasbourg. Its daily services of Holy Communion, Matins and Evensong had conformed precisely to the rules and regulations as set out in the rubrics of the Book of Common Prayer. With the advent of Simon Preston working in harness with Dean Carpenter, there was every prospect that musical standards would once again arise from the correct, if somewhat moribund level, at which they had been chugging along – that they would indeed flame up like a Pheonix from the ashes.

Indeed, for those first three years, this is just what happened. Not only did the choristers develop a fine tone and flexibility such as I had certainly never before heard in that building, but the lay vicars – as difficult a band to keep happy as their fellows in any other collegiate establishment – were one and all behind Simon in his endeavours. But with the arrival of Dean Michael Mayne it was not long before things began to creak at the seams. Psalms for the Day were no longer a *sine qua non*, and the language of the liturgy and of Bible readings were no more necessarily those of the established church. Sunday evenings would be taken up with a Taizé service beloved of the vice-Dean. There had, of course, been squalls at Westminster Abbey in the past, but this was no squall. It would have been healthier if it had been. It was decimation. The spat in 1901 between Dean Armitage Robinson and Canon Hensley Henson, as reported by T.F. Taylor in his biography of the former, makes for light reading in comparison.

The organist of the Abbey is, by statute, in absolute charge of the music to be sung at services. He chooses it and he trains the choir to sing it. So long as the services are from the Book of Common Prayer and adhere to its rubrics there is no problem. But a problem did now arise in that in 1980 Archbishop Runcie had officially launched the use of the *Alternative Service Book*. Mark well that word *Alternative*. It was to serve as an insidious and convenient shield for what was to become a near destruction of the very Church of England itself. But at this point, and with the retirement of Dean Carpenter, the musical authority of the Abbey Organist was reduced to a level of ridicule, for he no longer had the backing of the Church's fundamental literature upon which to base his musical practice. As dedicated artists and musicians, we do not compromise. Our goal is that of a perfection which as mere human beings we know we can never achieve. In 1987 Mr Preston resigned and the whole unsavoury story became revealed in the press reports of the time.

On 21st May of that year the Dean of Westminster wrote to *The Times* 'in view of the rumours and half-truths which are being circulated', saying that 'Mr Preston presented his resignation to the Dean and Chapter on the grounds that he wished to give more time to his professional career as a performer.' My own reaction to this statement was 'A likely tale!'. As a former cathedral organist and a long-standing friend of Simon Preston, I knew only too well and to my own everlasting pain that our careers and vocations had been in the performance of our duties as collegiate musicians and not in the transient world of mere recitalists and recording artists.

So what had gone wrong? Mr Preston went to the Abbey after twelve years at Christ Church, Oxford, and a previous term as assistant organist to Sir William McKie when the latter was Abbey organist. Therefore Mr Preston must have known that to which he was returning. Why should he change his mind? Thus it becomes relevant that on 15th May previous to the Dean's letter, the *Church Times* had already reported that 'it is acknowledged that winds of change at the Abbey have influenced his departure, even though there has been "no major row". A gradual move towards the modern liturgies has dismayed the master-musician, whose devotion centres on the classical settings. The ASB does not fit his music.' Therefore it is inevitable that the music goes overboard, because 'In the beginning was the word', and that is what the music was all about. And with the music go dignity, reverence, restraint, Manners that Makyth Man, self-respect. In come such travesties as the funeral for Diana, Princess of Wales, complete with its 'pop' song for her sung by Elton John, and all its implied insult to the Royal Family. But by this time Michael Mayne had retired and his successor was beginning to make his presence felt. And the most recent Royal marriage took place according to the rubrics of the Book of Common Prayer and was celebrated in St George's Chapel, Windsor Castle – which, together with St James' Palace, Hampton Court Palace and St Peter *ad Vincula* in the Tower of London, is a Royal Peculiar within the meaning of the act. Westminster Abbey is not, Queen Elizabeth I never having signed the relevant document.

In view of all this, and since Westminster Abbey does not come under any diocesan authority, this glorious place has in reality less status than the humblest parish church. Only by tradition is it used for the coronation of our Monarchs and for other great state occasions. Its newly appointed Organist, selected not by Her Majesty the Queen, but by a professionally engaged firm of head hunters, is a Roman Catholic – a man who has gained for himself a splendid reputation through his training of the choir at Westminster Cathedral. The Press suggest that this may lead to a few raised eyebrows. Why? Tallis and Byrd were both 'stiff papists' all their lives. They were also both Gentlemen of Her Majesty's Chapel Royal, and both contributed beyond price to the Canticle Settings and Anthem repertoire of the Church of England while continuing to compose and (by licence from Her Majesty) publish a vast quantity of superb music setting Latin words from the liturgy of the Catholic Church. That our choral foundations should ever be in any way desecrated, that they should ever be subjected to that Blairite frivolity termed 'Equality of the Sexes' would never have occurred to any of these people. Charity, that today much abused word, then meant what it said: loving kindness, which can work the most amazing transformations in us all. And the newly appointed Organist of Westminster Abbey, as an hereditary Catholic, will not – indeed, *cannot* – feel the pain as felt by such a one as Simon Preston.

At this point therefore one needs to ask, 'Who is the Head of the Church of England?' Nominally, but only nominally, it is the ruling Monarch. But we now have a 'constitutional' Monarchy. So the ultimate Head of Affairs is the Prime Minister. Today (2000) that is Mr Tony Blair, a man professing to be a practising member of the Church of England, married to a practising Catholic and with two children at the Oratory School. But to demonstrate upon what shabby ground our 'constitution' is built one needs only to read the following:

> Before the reign of William and Mary not only was the Monarch in fact the Head of the Church, but also the principal Officers of State were chosen by and were responsible to the Sovereign alone, and not to Parliament or to the nation at large. Such officers acted sometimes in concert with one another, but more often independently, and the fall of one did not, of necessity, involve that of the others, although all were liable to be dismissed at any moment.

> In 1693 the Earl of Sunderland recommended to William III [a Dutchman] the advisability of selecting a ministry from the political party which enjoyed a majority in the House of Commons, and the first united ministry was drawn in 1696 from the Whigs, to which party the King owed his throne ... The accession of George I, [a Hanoverian] who was unfamiliar with the English language, led to a disinclination on the part of the Sovereign to preside at meetings of his Ministers, and caused the appearance of a Prime Minister, a position first acquired by Robert Walpole in 1721, and retained by him without interruption for over twenty years. Thus, instead of Monarchical Government, came about Government by Party as we know it today.

(All this is plainly elucidated in *Whitaker's Almanack* for anyone who cares to read it.)

So the role of the Monarch became a constitutional one – cruelly, in many respects, little better than that of a rubber stamp. Evelyn Waugh provides a nice parody in his book *Vile Bodies*,[10] when the ex-King of Ruritania exclaims:

> It is one very extraordinary thing, your British Constitution. Me, I have never liked Prime Ministers. They talk and talk and then they talk more. 'Sir, you must sign that. Sir, you must go here and there. Sir, you must do up that button before you give audience to the black plenipotentiary from Liberia!' Pah! After the war my people give me the bird, yes; but they throw my Prime Minister out of the window ...

And even our people's President may meet his match: for it would seem that he suggested that for the future Her Majesty the Queen should travel to the State Opening of Parliament by motor car. Alas, he stubbed his toe, and Her Majesty has let it be known that she has no intention of relinquishing her much loved mode of transport – Coach and Horses. Seen in retrospect, perhaps it is the greatest tragedy that the Monarchy was not restored to its rightful position with the accession of Queen Victoria, notwithstanding the fact that she was but nineteen years of age at the time of her coronation. But Ministers had had a taste of power, and there was no way in which they were going to relinquish it.

Blair too has now had his taste of power, and its manifestations have proved not only true to form, but predictably so. Son of a respected Durham University professor, and himself a Durham cathedral school-boy, a public school man, an Oxford graduate and through a process of perfidious thinking, cool leader of New Labour, he is supported in the interests of equal opportunities by a vast band of parliamentary females each and every one, of course, subject to the Whip (*pace* the Marquis de Sade!). It is this combined and carefully dragooned host which now holds the reins. They represent 'a certain sort of feminism which is so keen to advance women's equal rights with men that it refuses to recognise basic biological differences between the sexes.'[11]

They even make demands for a crêche to be provided in the House of Commons so that the tiresome business of little children may be resolved. Would Blair have become a cathedral schoolboy from such a background as that which his parliamentary females now propose for their offspring? And does being a cathedral schoolboy really matter as long as in later life one has a guitar upon which to strum? After all, cathedrals represent an area seriously in need of adjustment in terms of sexual equality, and in all ways and in all things sexual equality must be established even if it means flying in the face of nature. One's honesty to God may fail, but it is honesty honed to the politic which must come first – with its ultimate reward of being Dictator of the Lowest Common Denominator.

But the trouble is that however blind one's eye may be, in the end God fails to play the game. He will not be mocked. 'Male and Female created He them'.[12] At the time of birth a baby is either a boy or it is a girl. It is either male or female. To seek to establish that the sexes are equal is to indulge in a form of blasphemy: for they are not. They are complementary, as created by Almighty God. Thus, assuming that there is no artificial and self-gainful interference on the part of either parent, each sex proceeds on an individually normal course from childhood to puberty.

For a boy, the culmination of this halcyon period is manifested by, amongst other things, a gradual or sudden change in the singing and speaking voice. The upper registers progressively diminish and frequently, for a period, the voice is out of control. As with a girl, physical changes gradually come about, though these are of a widely different character. For the boy who has, from the age of seven or eight, been a scientifically trained cathedral chorister, it is the end of a highly specialised way of life. Throughout the age of pubescence he will gradually and with considerable mental pain grope his way towards maturity and early manhood. With care in the late teens there may be the makings of a singing voice to be sympathetically trained. Gaucheness and clumsiness will begin to disappear.

The girl, too, goes through a phased sequence of development, but it is one of an entirely different nature in every respect. When I was at the Royal Academy of Music as an organ scholar, there was a young pianist of outstanding natural musicianship called Dorothy Bond. But her innate desire was to be a singer, and certainly there was every indication that she possessed the makings of a voice of extraordinary range. However, the senior female singing professor of the time told her that she must be patient and that she would not touch such a delicate vocal instrument until Dorothy was twenty years old. Professor Evelyn Langston proved to be right and produced in Dorothy Bond an utterly amazing coloratura soprano – so amazing indeed that Beecham took her up and she worked with him in many of his concerts. Sadly, like Dennis Brain, she was killed while still in her twenties in a motoring smash. But where would the makings of that voice have been if, as a young girl, she had fallen into the clutches of such as are the present organists of more than one of our cathedrals? As to those clergy who presume to support such organists, they know not what they are saying.

A prize example of this latter point must surely be that as exemplified by Canon Paul Lucas, Precentor of Wells Cathedral (as reported in *The Sunday Independent* on 20th December 1998). Apparently he felt that only the *cognoscenti* of the cathedral would be able to tell that a girl choir was to sing on Christmas Day. One wonders if, perchance, he included Almighty God among the *cognoscenti*, or whether the lure of financial aid from the Department of Education and Employment had been successful in blinding him to this unfashionable proposition. As to the heartbreak of those choristers who were to be thus displaced and whose voices would have broken by the Christmas of 1999, not a word was said.

Nevertheless, I am not suggesting in any way that the female voice does not begin to have its place in the right sphere at the right time. My reflections on my fellow student, Dorothy Bond, make this abundantly clear. But 'what is truth' said jesting Pilate; and, as we know, he was not prepared to stay and hear the answer. The truth is that were the sexes *not* complementary there would have been *no* Maria Callas to sing the name part in Donizetti's *Lucia di Lammermoor*; *no* Lisa della Casa to sing 'Arabella' in the Strauss opera of that name; nor would we ever have had the wonderful 'Falstaff' of either Tito Gobbi or Geraint Evans, or the shuddering icy grip of Chaliapin's 'Death of Boris' in Moussorgsky's opera. Not one of these roles is interchangeable. As to the sheer *joie de vivre* and extrovert gymnastics of Sylvia Geszty as Zerbinetta in Strauss's *Ariadne*, the memory thrills me to this day.

Ultimately one cannot, in sanity, support in any way the current fetish of feminism be it manifested by Parliament, bishops, deans, canons, or any of their clerical brethren. Schools, colleges, universities and all those other establishments that are attempting this are simply blundering up a blind alley and show that, at some point in time, a dreadful malaise has come upon them. This is not to presuppose any psychological dislike of young girls. It merely demonstrates that they, in their innocence, are being exploited in totally false situations by their seniors who, committed to their feminist persuasions, now undertake to 'play God'. It is not young girls, but these latter people who stand on the brink of that terrible perdition: 'For whoso shall offend one of these little ones, it were better for him that he had a millstone about his neck, and that he were cast into the depths of the sea.' In order to preserve any decent sort of civilisation, it is imperative that these vociferous and easy word-spinning seducers be withstood. They play a dirty game, and for every inch they are given, they will certainly take an ell*, and yet another young child will be 'offended'.

However, lest one should think that all this is a new and therefore somewhat trivial phenomenon that will simply pass away, it is possible to cite two widely separated examples of its continuing presence. Aristophanes, who lived some four hundred years before the time of Christ, saw the concept of feminism as mere comedy – hence his play *Lysistrata*. Many years later, Jane Austen, the daughter of a country rector, used it as a basis for ridicule in her novel *Pride and Prejudice* – demonstrating what an appalling mess Mrs Bennet contrived to make of her family, in the face of her browbeaten and too easy-going husband. And in presuming to write such things, I myself am now breaking the law of the land and inviting prosecution on the grounds of sexual discrimination! This very fact surely proves that the feminists *know* that they have not a weak, but an untenable case. Thus they flee at the suggestion of basic but

---

*A former measure of length used mainly for textiles; normally forty-five inches in England and thirty-seven inches in Scotland.

unpalatable truth. It was marvellously demonstrated in the Crockford scandal of the 1980s.

Every year, Crockford's Clerical Directory was published with a Preface that was by tradition anonymous and fearlessly outspoken. No one knew who the author might be excepting the Editor himself. But with the ever growing disintegration of and disagreements among the clerical hierarchy, the Preface of 1987 aroused a storm without precedent. A storm demonstrating the sudden panic of finding that there seemed to be no one at the steering wheel – that perhaps the great ship was suddenly being scuttled – that everything was being allowed to drift in all directions at once – that somebody had had the temerity to demand: 'What *is* the Church of England?'

Reactions were perhaps predictable. The then Archbishop of Canterbury saw fit to nail his colours to the fence. The Archbishop of York set up what can only be described as a witch-hunt worthy of mediaeval times. He was going to get his man, and of course the Press were only too happy to provide their readership with full reports. So a priest was driven to annihilation and the Editor of Crockford's was forbidden ever to publish another Preface. The offending Preface was hurriedly withdrawn from all copies of the Directory that were to be distributed to the clergy in general and the hierarchy of the church came out of the affair in a manner recalling to one's mind the behaviour of the Gaderene Swine.

Panic plays strange games. If the Church of England had been allowed to remain what it purported to be through its books of 1549, 1552 and 1662, with its Book of Common Prayer, its uncompromising rubrics, its Authorised Version of the Holy Bible, none of this would ever have happened. The Reverend Gareth Bennett would never have been hounded to his death. As William Oddie suggests on the opening page of his book, *The Crockford File*, the whole unsavoury business simply demonstrated the death of the Anglican Mind.[13]

By the time of Dr Bennett's death in the December of 1987, the Alternative Service Book's usage had spread so widely that in most places it was regarded as the Accepted Service Book, invariably partnered by the New English Bible. But the practice did not seem to be working. Congregations appeared to be falling off. In panic, it seemed that the only way to rectify this was to give the people what they wanted. So in many churches Evensong was dropped, perhaps to be replaced by an Evening Service – the latter as convenient a euphemism as the title Family Service for whatever might be enacted in the morning. But it seemed that the ordinary man in the street was not impressed by this patronising treatment. We all know the worth of the person who endeavours to be all things to all men. We also know that that is no description of Our Lord. We are seeing the strangulation of a God-given Church, a Church that was formerly rich beyond compare in God-given culture in all its diverse forms; a Church such as may 'Dissolve me into ecstasies, And bring all Heav'n before mine eyes.' No wonder that, as a small boy, I wondered if the interior of that Gothic church at Ambleteuse was perhaps a manifestation of heaven on earth.

One requires to remember that 'the first instinct of the gentleman is respect for the past with all it connotes of art and religion and thought.' But 'the first instinct of the educated unfit is to hate and destroy the past.'[14] So, emanating from a structure headed by a former cathedral schoolboy, the Department of Education and Employment can say

> that there is ample scope for widening the opportunities for a chorister education to include girls. Salisbury and Wells Cathedral Choir Schools were selected to be founder beneficiaries of the Choir Schools Scholarship Scheme because, amongst other things, they were taking the innovative step of establishing girl choirs . . . We believe that there is room for all types and *all tastes* (my italics) in our choral heritage.

So the whole matter becomes exposed for what it truly is: an insidiously manoeuvred political and hierarchical confidence trick. There are high-handed insolent frauds and there are creeping and sneaking ones. And today, in order to promote motivation that will be a political success, one requires to be a master of both techniques – not just a committed and self-deceiving fraud, but a hypocrite. Thus the disappearance of the Book of Common Prayer with its unique heritage of glorious music; thus the loss of the Authorised Version of the Holy Bible; thus the desecration of church buildings, shabbily refurnished in terms of 'get together' meetings which no right thinking man can view without suffering both pain and embarrassment.

Meanwhile the easy way out becomes the accepted thing. It has been easy to close one theological college after another because of an apparent shortage of vocations. It has been easy to open the doors to women who, in the present climate, have naturally not been backward in coming forward. Beware the legal offence of sexual discrimination. That the Church might have exercised a little faith does not accord with today's fashions. God gave man free-will. It does not have to be 'Thy will be done'. There is a choice. And the consequences are now speaking for themselves.

Inevitably of course there is an impasse, for Almighty God can no longer be seen as being politically correct. He failed in that He created the sexes as being not equal, but complementary. So state schools and many of our hitherto admired public schools are now co-educational. By token of which, cathedral choir schools must become co-educational with their terms geared not to the Church's Calendar but to terms imposed by the State itself. In this year 2000 we can view a repressive iconoclasm eating its way into an actual literary, clerical, ritual and musical heritage which was bequeathed to us in England over a period amounting to some nine hundred years. We also celebrate the tenth anniversary of the inception of this practice of the 'girl choir' when it was set up by Richard Seal, the then organist of Salisbury. We may look from Exeter to York, from Ripon to Manchester, to Peterborough, to Southwark, almost to where you will, and so the sorry tale goes on. Now, the latest establishment to 'get with it': Winchester.

Winchester, the one-time capital of Wessex where in 827 Egbert was crowned first king of all England. Winchester, where Edward the Confessor was crowned. Winchester, where William the Conqueror and some of his successors also were crowned in addition to their London coronations. Winchester, regarded by them as being their second capital. Winchester, which unleashed its girl choir in the June of 1999. BBC TV requested permission and came to interview me at my home.

On matters of this sort the BBC remains impartial. Having arranged lighting and camera-sound equipment, I was asked to relax in my favourite armchair and to express my views generally and in particular on what had come about at Winchester. Mentioning that it was surely a very sad way for that foundation to be celebrating its 900th anniversary, I also found it heartbreaking to see yet another cathedral wilfully destroying its sole *raison d'être*: *that* being

> by its own beauty and by the religious service held within it, to give contin-
> uous witness to the things unseen and eternal, and to offer continuous and
> reverent worship to Almighty God. *To this supreme object all others must
> be subsidiary.*[15]

I was asked just one question: did I think that there would ever be a recovery from what had come about? Of course I am sure that there will be. The Church has been in very deep waters before now. But the recovery may not happen in my lifetime.

The BBC team then set off for Winchester for the remainder of their programme, but I was advised as to when transmission would take place and so was eventually able to see and hear the final product. Following on my own observations came the Very Reverend the Dean of Winchester presenting precisely the obverse side of the coin. I do not know the Dean, but I would guess that, whatever his private convictions, he must beware the law against sexual discrimination. Were he to offend against this he might even find himself in prison. One cannot serve both God and Mammon; one must make one's choice; it is called being diplomatic. Archbishop Cranmer chose to serve God and the Church of England; he was duly burned at the stake by the Roman Catholic Queen Mary.

The programme continued with the Winchester girl choir in rehearsal. The rehearsal was not taken by the cathedral organist, but by his recently appointed female assistant. I found this interesting. The man trains the choristers but a woman is required to attempt to train the girls who, unlike the choristers, cover an age range from ten years to sixteen. Sexual equality would appear to be posing some sort of a problem! It is only fair to say that the whole episode was utterly pathetic – indeed, embarrassing. That poor assistant organist trying in vain to make bricks without straw while the girls, red cassocked and white ruffed, gasped and strained for they knew not what. But doubtless Mr Blair will, if he lasts, see that they get some financial support in line with Salisbury and Wells. Today's young innocent faces are the votes he wants tomorrow.

To set against this it is a happiness to learn that the choristers and lay clerks of Canterbury Cathedral still sing the psalms for the day as set out in the translations of Miles Coverdale in the Book of Common Prayer. But it is hardly amusing that in this same year Archbishop Carey should see fit to close the Lambeth Conference *not* with a prayer of thanksgiving to Our Lady, but by holding hands with everybody and partaking in a vociferous rendering of 'Waltzing Matilda'. However, I have yet to finish with 1999, for not everything was negative.

It was in the June of that year that Peter Giles, the Chairman of CDTCC*, asked me to come and give a talk at their annual general meeting, to be held at St Andrew-by-the-Wardrobe in the city of London. It was many years since I had been in the Square Mile, and when my taxi crossed Blackfriars Bridge and stopped we seemed to be nowhere. In the days before the war I had often been around the City, either taking a solid-tyred and open-topped General omnibus (if it rained you put up your umbrella) or simply walking from street to street. Everywhere there were the spires, towers and belfrys of Wren's wonderful churches crowning the city buildings – some of them Georgian, some Victorian. In particular I recalled St Stephen, Walbrook, with its central dome and its East and West, North and South short projections – as it were creating the shape of a Latin cross. It carried a majesty which somehow became completely lost in the vast and less disciplined spaces of St Paul's Cathedral.

But on this day in mid-summer, everything had gone. The last I had seen of it was from some twenty miles away on that terrible night as it blazed away during the Blitz. Now all I saw was one faceless and towering block of concrete business building after another. It was all soulless. What was I doing there?

Yet they are still there, each one (or at least most of them) simply

*Campaign for the Defence of the Traditional Cathedral Choir.

concealed by the bland fronts of Big Business; and walking round an obscure corner, there was Wren's beautifully restored St Andrew-by-the-Wardrobe. I entered to be greeted by many old friends and to find myself surrounded by many people whom I had never seen before. Not only that, but the church itself was used; and I now learn from an article by the Reverend Peter Mullen, Rector of St Michael's, Cornhill, and co-editor of *Faking It*, that the many city churches *are* used and are crowded by congregations thirsty for the Book of Common Prayer and the true Church of England.

To my great pleasure, my illustrated talk (the gist of which lies in this book) was received with enthusiasm, only one person making a hurried departure at the end; and, strangely enough, the police were not waiting for me when I left the building. But still the fear lingers with me. We are talking to a closed society – and I have by no means come to the end of my song. In the words of Dylan Thomas it is necessary that one 'Rage – rage against the dying of the light.'

It is gratifying to see that the rage is beginning to break out from an hitherto unexpected quarter: 'President' Blair's own MPs (the *Daily Telegraph*, Saturday 21st August 1999). They propose that he should be brought before a Commons select committee (something which has never previously been required of a sitting Prime Minister) to give a full account of his style of government, including the ever growing number of 'unaccountable' political advisers in Downing Street. The present Archbishop of York may say that should a female ever become a 'bishop', then he would step down and return to being a parish priest. But that simply closes the stable door after the horse has bolted. Usurpation starts at the top and flows down. Unless steps are taken to stem the tide, we finish up with a dictatorship enhanced with what can be no more than a joke-monarchy. It would seem that this insidious programme has now reached a stage where those sane members of Mr Blair's party consider that he should be stopped in his tracks. What sort of a brazen hierarchy do we now have, that it dares to dice with the truth?

When in 1980 the Alternative Service Book was formally launched by Archbishop Runcie, it was intended that it should have an initial life of twenty years which period now expires. The Prime Minister at that time was a non-conformist so, in all good conscience, the matter cannot have been one of fundamental import to her. But with the advent of the so-called Millennium we are to be faced with the next great step forward – as announced by the Bishop of Salisbury, a new liturgy entitled 'Common Worship.'

Of course as far as the Church of England is concerned, the use of the Book of Common Prayer is still mandatory. The law has never been rescinded. The Book of Common Prayer remains the official Prayer

Book of the Church of England. But from Advent 2000 a new book called Common Worship (which contains much material from the BCP) would be available to be used in parallel or as an alternative. Once again, some sort of desperate hope to fill our churches. Yet again, this panic . . . this lack of faith . . . this refusal to accept that a house divided against itself will fall. Always this implied suggestion that the authorised Church of England need no longer be taken as being the final word. There is no longer any need to be a fully paid up member. If one 'shop' does not provide the goods precisely as one would wish, one can always find another 'shop' around the corner. For the third time (that is since the specious introduction of the Series A and B rites) the hierarchy propose to have another tedious shot. *Sempre la stessa musica*: 'As you like it' or 'What you will'.

This of course is no sane answer to a panic engendered situation – that of a frightened and faithless hierarchy too muddled to be able to exercise any kind of authority. All that can be done by such people is to betray the Church while claiming not to desert it. They also, of course, betray the Royal Family, Her Majesty the Queen as *Defensor Fidei*, and the Royal Peculiars adhering faithfully to the Prayer Book.

But such things did not happen before Robert Walpole became the first Prime Minister. Henry VIII (the first English monarch to receive in perpetuity the Papal honour of *Defensor Fidei*) was prompt in his dispatching of Cardinal Wolsey who, amongst other things, was at one time drawing the emoluments from no less than five vacant bishoprics. And Pius V's eventual excommunication of Elizabeth I achieved no more than an English closing of ranks. But now, since the time when William the Dutchman agreed to government by that political party having a majority, and the establishment of a Prime Minister on behalf of King George I, everything has existed in a state of jeopardy. A run of political parties constituted in the main by gentlemen managed to maintain some sort of *status quo*. It is amazing that it should have lasted for as long as it did, for it only requires the right man to gain power at the wrong time, or the wrong man to gain power at the right time, and devastation must inevitably follow. This so-called age of the Common Man is not only a lie – it is an impossibility. Were we to be truly classless, the machinery just would not work. It would perforce simply stand and stagnate.

A simple and totally unemotional example may be gleaned from the old GWR – God's Wonderful Railway, as it was known. Put a Castle locomotive to work in a marshalling yard and two things would at once happen: a tremendous fuel consumption to no purpose and immediate derailment because of sharp radii. Put a Pannier Tank to haul a West Country Express and within no time fuel from the small bunker would be totally consumed and even over the short distance covered, no speed of significance would have been achieved.

Mr Blair is, I fear, in the wrong class. He may have been to public school. Both the locomotives mentioned above were created at Swindon works. The locomotives, when doing the right jobs, were marvels. Mr Blair, his audacity apart, is scarcely so to be described, but he may succeed in making one cringe. In the 1999 opening of Parliament Her Majesty Queen Elizabeth II had to read as the first item in Her 'speech' the planned machinery for ridding the House of Lords from all who were hereditary peers. Her reading was not even heard in the traditional respectful silence, but was punctuated by gleeful sniggers from certain members of Mr Blair's Party.

William of Wykeham gave to his college as its motto the simple reminder: *Manners Makyth Man*. One may look to Mr Blair's party in vain. I am sure that he has his own ideas as to what eventually is to happen to the House of Windsor. And as to the non-conformist element now suppurating the Church of England: 'Better leave the rest unsaid.'[16]

Chapter XV

Retrospection
Dans la forêt de Septembre

When, in March 1937, Charles-Marie Widor lay in his final illness, he said to Marcel Dupré, 'I cannot complain for I have had a wonderful life.'[17] I would without any hesitation echo Widor's words, even though it is not given to me to know when my life will end; only that one day the Hound of Heaven will overtake me. Were it not for all that I inherited from my mother and father, and which was so caringly nurtured by my aunt Nora, I could never have reached those moments of inspiration which led to the creation of the Renaissance Singers and the Renaissance Society. And were it not for the impact of the Renaissance Singers during their first nine years, together with my opportunities to work so extensively with John Whitworth, I should never have become Organist of Ely Cathedral. Nor did the miracle finish there. In Dr Arthur Wills I was blessed with the ideal assistant organist, for his vision was large enough to see that as far as the Chapter and the Choir were concerned it must never be apparent which of us was playing for any given service or part of a service. In matters of accompaniment there must be one style only, and he unfailingly followed in the manner that I wished. Not that he was any cypher. His bursts of glorious improvisation and his bravura voluntaries all testified to that. By 1958, Simon Preston was still a Cambridge organ scholar. It was only right that Wills should succeed me.

Another, and to me, equally great gift was that I had been able to combine the glories of the Ely choristers with the achievements of the Renaissance Singers, thus producing a conjunction of similarities which became famed throughout the country. And when I had been so nearly obliterated – a victim of alcoholism – still the Hound was after me and decreed that I must go on through *Cantores in Ecclesia*. So I find myself indebted to more people, places and things than I can ever hope to recall. Indeed, as we approached the moot point of the so-called Millennium, avoiding the question of whether it be Julian or Gregorian, admitting that temporal accuracy was impossible and furthermore did not matter in any serious sense, I merely saw a vast expenditure of money on an ultimate nothing. The Great Dome! How utterly pathetic, as I see again 'high over all, the Cross and the Ball on the riding redoubtable Dome of St Paul's';[18] the Octagon of Ely Cathedral, the crouched vaulting of the nave of Tewkesbury Abbey. I have no idea what tomorrow may bring, either to myself or to that Church of England which I learned by so circuitous a route to love. Life is sufficient unto the day, in every sense. The end is to be found in the Book of Revelations. Ely Cathedral and its miracles of the 1950s are for ever ingrained in my very being.

Notes and References

1. *Pickwick Papers* Charles Dickens Centennial Edition, Heron Books, Preface, p. 17.
2. *Faking it* (1998) The Social Affairs Unit.
3. *Decline and Fall* (1928) Evelyn Waugh, Chapman and Hall Ltd.
4. In spite of this curious prejudice, the Chaplain as a matter of course always cele-brated a 7.00 a.m. Requiem Eucharist on 2nd November, All Souls Day. When my mother came to hear of this she was both furious and disgusted but then her family came from County Wicklow.
5. Michael Watts was later to become Director of Music at Ardingly; his sister, Helen was an opera singer who appeared at, amongst other places, Glyndebourne.
6. *vide* Fritz Busch and the recitatives at Glyndebourne!
7. Surely written not for organ but for pedal-cembalo.
8. *A Little Learning* (1964) Evelyn Waugh, cap VII, Chapman and Hall Ltd.
9. Brother of the Eric Waddams who had joined the staff so greatly to my benefit at Ellesmere.
10. *Vile Bodies* (1930) Evelyn Waugh, Chapman and Hall Ltd.
11. *Faking it – ut supra –* cap I p. 17.
12. Genesis 1:27.
13. For a full account see *The Crockford File* (1989) William Oddie, Hamish Hamilton, London.
14. *Sinister Street* (1939) Compton MacKenzie, cap VI.
15. The Cathedral Commission (1927).
16. *Bitter Lemons*, Lawrence Durrell, Faber & Faber.
17. *Dupré Raconte* (Paris 1972).
18. *England their England* (1941) A.G. Macdonell, The Reprint Society, London.

I am grateful to the National Monuments Record for their permission to reproduce copyright material – the photographs of The Royal Academy of Music and The Brompton Oratory; St Peter's, Eaton Square; Christ Church, Woburn Square; the organ, Framlingham Church and Christ Church, St Leonards. The photograph of the organ at Tewkesbury Abbey is by A. F. Kersting and used with permission.